MIGRANT SONG

Migrant Song

POLITICS AND PROCESS
IN CONTEMPORARY
CHICANO LITERATURE

TERESA MCKENNA

UNIVERSITY OF TEXAS PRESS
Austin

First edition, 1997

Requests for permission to reproduce material from this work
should be sent to Permissions, University of Texas Press, Box 7819,
Austin, TX 78713-7819.

Credits for previously published material appear on pages xi – xii.

⊗ The paper used in this publication meets the minimum
requirements of American National Standard for Information
Sciences—Permanence of Paper for Printed Library Materials,
ANSI Z39.48-1984.

LIBRARY OF CONGRESS CATALOGING-IN-PUBLICATION DATA

McKenna, Teresa.
    Migrant song : politics and process in contemporary Chicano
literature / Teresa McKenna. — 1st ed.
        p.   cm.
    Includes bibliographical references and index.
    ISBN 978-0-292-75188-0

    1. American literature—Mexican American authors—History and
criticism.   2. American literature—20th century—History and
criticism.   3. Emigration and immigration in literature.   4. Politics
and literature—United States—History—20th century.   5. Politics
and literature—Mexico—History—20th century.   6. Literature and
society—United States—History—20th century.   7. Literature and
society—Mexico—History—20th century.   8. Mexican Americans—
Intellectual life.   9. Mexican Americans in literature.   I. Title.
PS153.M4M55   1997
810.9'86872'09045—dc20   96-25379

A mis abuelas
Cruz Santibáñez y Inez Fonseca Amescua
y a mis padres
José de la Luz McKenna y Concepción McKenna
quienes me dieron vida y gozo
y
a Arturo Islas
quien compartió conmigo la generosidad de su espíritu

PARTO DE PALABRA

Triste voz
bitter sweat
between ocean waves

formando orígenes
entre apocalipsis

Música triste
erupts horizons
que partan luz

Contents

Acknowledgments

When we were children, my abuelita Cruz would sit us all in the small living room of her wood-slatted house and tell us stories. By the light of the high naked light bulb she would tell, play, and sing for us the tales, games, and songs of her long-abandoned home, Silao, Guanajuato. Later I understood that those nights connected me to a much larger story, one of revolution, from which my grandmothers, alone, had fled, bringing their small children over the border and into another land; one of struggle, in which they had protected their families from hunger, drought, and influenza. But those nights at 821 Pioneer Avenue in Wilmington, California, commenced for me a song of migration that has since fueled my political and academic work.

One of my abuelita's favorite games was one that was designed to make her small charges fall asleep. We would sit in a row on the long couch and she would sit in her chair off to the side. We were to play as if our hands were loaves of bread, so she instructed us to cross our arms and to sway back and forth to the rhythmic song she sang: "Dormir, dormir, cantan los gallos de San Agustín." After repeating the song three times, she would ask, "¿Tan, tan, ya está el pan?" She would make us show our hands and touch to see if they were warm. Inevitably they were not. She would claim, "No, todavía no. Todavía no llega el panadero." And we would go back to our crossed arms and our swaying to the song. El panadero never came (although sleep did). But for me the song continues to this day. The process of baking that bread is one I carry with me metaphorically as I too have taken out my work and have exclaimed over and over again, "No, todavía no." Writing and producing this book has been a process that began in some uncertain moment when I first wakened to the struggles for civil rights in the sixties; it is a process that continues to this day as I act within the arenas of academic life. I have come to realize that whether the bread is baked or not is not totally relevant; the process of its being made is.

Several years ago I sat in another living room, one that had the glow of the sunset on its walls and the sound of gentle breezes ruffling the leaves of well-tended plants out in the patio. It was the graceful and warm domain of Arturo Islas, my friend and mentor. He read for me passages from his next book, *Migrant Souls*, in particular the part where we are told how Mama Chona's husband had died and how her last child had been born. The family was fleeing war-torn revolutionary Mexico and at this point in the story was caught on the border. Jesus Angel was struck down by the train that had brought them to Juárez; as he lay dying, in the cot next to him Chona lay giving birth to her son. As the life flowed out of the man, life insisted itself in Chona and the child was born: "Jesus stopped breathing the moment he heard your brother's first cry into the world. Only seconds before, he said, 'It goes on, Chona. It goes on.' He meant life, I'm certain of it" (Islas 1990, p. 232). As my abuelitas Cruz and Inez taught me much about patience and persistence through their lives and their stories, Arturo Islas taught me about the continuation of life and the struggle to produce fitting stories of our passing. In a small way this book attempts to honor their lives and their teaching.

Through my grandmothers, Cruz Santibáñez and Inez Fonseca Amescua, and my parents, José de la Luz McKenna and Concepción McKenna, I was given the spirit and the means to understand the beauty and the struggles of life. I owe them my life and work. Because of Arturo Islas I began to understand the immense satisfaction of personal and public life. He is with me still. And to good and loyal friends I give my heartfelt thanks for their constant encouragement, their unfailing support, and their wise counsel along the way—José Limón, Juan Gómez-Quiñones, Devra Weber, Pat Mora, Elizabeth Forsyth, Rolando Hinojosa, and Vincent Cheng. Especially I thank Raymond E. Castro for sharing with me the pain and felicity of the process of seeing this manuscript come to light and for his loving and generous friendship.

So many people have helped to make this project possible. I appreciate the encouragement by José David Saldívar to collect my work into this volume and the constant urging of Sonia Saldívar-Hull to publish it. I owe a great debt to Elizabeth Forsyth for her intellectual advice and editorial help. I also extend deep thanks to Nellie Ayala-Reyes, Kevin Ennis, B. K. Watson, Wade Thompson-Harper, and Doris D'Amico, who together assured that this manuscript was completed. I could not have done the bulk of the work for this volume without the support of Arturo Madrid and the Tomás Rivera Center for Policy Studies and the support of the Ford Foundation Postdoctoral Fellowship for Minorities, as well as the University of

Texas at Austin and the Center for Mexican American Studies. I also extend my thanks to Stanford University and the Chicano Fellows Program for the intellectual environment of those Chicano Faculty Roundtables where Renato Rosaldo and Tomás Ybarra-Frausto helped me to think through many of the ideas in this volume. I also give my thanks to Dr. Américo Paredes for his generous intellectual leadership. Most especially I thank Marga Cottino-Jones, whose example as a scholar and a teacher still guides me.

I always return to my family: to my sisters, Amelia McKenna and Irene McKenna, and my brothers, Joseph McKenna and David McKenna. Together we have come to understand and to appreciate the bonds of our family and the love that sustains us all. With them and my parents and grandparents I learned that Mexico and Wilmington form the core of our histories. We share those histories and stories with the new generation, with Nichol Marie, Amy Elizabeth, Sara Inez, David Robert, and Ryan. It is for them and with them that the song goes on.

CREDITS FOR PREVIOUSLY PUBLISHED MATERIAL

An earlier version of Chapter 2 was published in *Criticism in the Borderlands: Studies in Chicano Literature, Culture, and Ideology*, ed. Héctor Calderón and José David Saldívar (Durham, N.C.: Duke University Press, 1991), pp. 181–202. Reprinted by permission.

"Emplumada" and "Visions of Mexico While at a Writing Symposium in Port Townsend, Washington" are reprinted from EMPLUMADA, by Lorna Dee Cervantes, by permission of the University of Pittsburgh Press. © 1981 by Lorna Dee Cervantes.

Selections from "Al pozo con Bruno Cano" from *Estampas del Valle* by Rolando Hinojosa (1994) and selections from "Bruno Cano: Lock, Stock, and Bbl." from *The Valley* by Rolando Hinojosa (1983) are reprinted by permission of the publisher, Bilingual Press/Editorial Bilingüe, Arizona State University, Tempe, Arizona.

"With a Polka in His Hand" by Evangelina Vigil-Pinon is reprinted with permission from the publisher of *Thirty an' Seen a Lot* (Houston: Arte Público Press, 1985).

"Borders," "Desert Women," and "Sonrisas" by Pat Mora are reprinted with permission from the publisher of *Borders* (Houston: Arte Público Press – University of Houston, 1986).

"Unrefined," "Illegal Alien," "Legal Alien," and "For Georgia O'Keefe" by Pat Mora are reprinted with permission from the publisher of *Chants* (Houston: Arte Público Press – University of Houston, 1984).

Excerpt from Jimmy Santiago Baca, *Immigrants in Our Own Land*, copyright © 1982 by Jimmy Santiago Baca, reprinted by permission of New Directions Pub. Corp.

Excerpts from *The Elements of San Joaquín* reprinted by permission of Gary Soto.

Excerpts from *Hunger of Memory* by Richard Rodriguez reprinted by permission of David R. Godine, Publisher, Inc. Copyright © 1982 by Richard Rodriguez.

"Poem in Lieu of Preface" by Alurista reprinted by permission of the author.

"Crítica for an arse poeticus" by Ricardo Sánchez reprinted from *Hechizospells* (Los Angeles: Chicano Studies Center Publications, UCLA, 1976).

Excerpts from *Borderlands / La Frontera: The New Mestiza* © 1987 by Gloria Anzaldúa. Reprinted with permission from Aunt Lute Books (415) 826-1300.

Excerpts from "Raw Experience" by Cherríe Moraga reprinted from *Loving in the War Years* with permission from the publisher, South End Press, 116 Saint Botolph Street, Boston, MA 02115, and Cherríe Moraga.

MIGRANT SONG

formando orígenes
entre apocalipsis

Parto
de palabra

THE MANY BIRTHS

OF THE MIGRANT SONG

In Spanish, parto means birth; in the poem that forms the epigram to this book, it refers to the birth of the word, the aesthetic communicative gesture of a people. I chose this metaphor to represent the development of Chicano literature because parto connotes the process of birthing: the dialectical interplay of openings and closings that produces life. The metaphor underscores a process, or diachronic profile, that must be separated from a simply chronological perspective: a process refers to discrete periods of cause and effect in which diachronic and synchronic elements meet to produce qualitative change, while a chronology refers to a linear progression. Anthropologists have used the term "processual" to describe processes that mark movement or change in society. It includes dramatistic analysis: the isolation of units of human activity into analogs of stage or performance. Most importantly, processual studies emphasize the complex, dynamic nature of human interaction. The processes under analysis might take the form of discrete moments or progressive duration. Through case studies of the various genres, this volume examines the processual quality of Chicano literature as it is informed by political activity.

These essays represent more than ten years of critical study. They correspond to my own reflection on diverse subjects at various political and critical moments and thus present discrete and at times competing approaches and perspectives. Yet each examination proceeds from the central critical assumption that Chicano literature arises out of social, political, and psychological conflict and that the processes of development of the literature are inextricably embedded in this fact. I have chosen to let my own processual world as critic parallel the process I am endeavoring to explore in these essays. The literature and the ways in which we talk about it are governed by similar configurations of history and event.

This perspective is grounded in the assumption that the social world, of which literature and literary theory are a part, is a world in becoming, not a world in being. This is not a new idea, to be sure. Others as diverse as Karl Marx, Emile Durkheim, Henri Bergson, and Victor Turner, to name only a few in modern times, have elaborated complex theories based on this observation. They share a common understanding that the process is advanced through a conflictual social interrelatedness, which can be labeled political, and that human social life is the producer and the product of time, to use Victor Turner's terms.

The complex interpretive structures that arise from these ideas have fueled much modern social and political thought and have sparked reconsideration of concepts such as nation, history, and literature. Victor Turner (1974, p. 32), who began to reconsider his view of primitive societies from this perspective, described his findings as follows: "With my conviction as to the dynamic character of social relations I saw movement as much as structure, persistence as much as change, indeed, persistence as a striking aspect of change."

Migrant Song, the title of this volume, embraces the movement and persistence that accompany the processual events affecting indigenous and Mexican peoples in the geographical area now called Mexico and the United States. The reference to migrants captures the constantly changing political structures and social and geopolitical spaces that accompany migration, while the peoples' cultural response in song attests to their persistence and permanence even in the midst of change. In this book I show that Chicano literary activity develops in a dialectical fashion and examine the historical and political nature of the processes of the literature as they are tied to conflict, that fundamental element of social intercourse.

In Chapter 1, I critically appraise the evolution of Chicano literature from oral forms and argue that migration is an appropriate root metaphor for Chicano writers, assessing where it was spawned and why it has continued to remain so dominant. Most importantly, I develop the notion that Chicano literature has developed out of social conflict and a reaction to political events. The ramifications of these facts are explored in detail in the following chapters.

In Chapter 2, I analyze the importance of the corrido, a form of narrative song, in the development of Chicano poetry. I look specifically at a series of corridos published in *El Grito del Norte*, a community newspaper from Española, New Mexico, which were written after two community activists were murdered in the early 1970s. Analysis of how the structural aspects of the corrido changed from oral to print forms gives way to a look at these new forms as aspects of a larger processual unit, the social drama. This perspective brings the analysis of the Canales/Córdova corridos within a larger rhetorical presentation in which the conflict within the community is shown to be causally linked to the total configuration of reportage, corrido, poem, and testimonio, in the newspaper presentation. This analysis is key to understanding the significant shift of Chicano poetry from its oral origins to the fundamentally print form we have today.

In Chapter 3, I focus on Richard Rodriguez's controversial autobiography as a means to address the problematics of presenting the self in Chicano literature. This discussion advances through a comparative analysis with other ethnic American autobiographers: N. Scott Momaday, Maya Angelou, and Maxine Hong Kingston. I borrowed the title of this chapter—"On Lies, Secrets, and Silence"—from Adrienne Rich because it brings to mind the attributes that account for the uniqueness and problems of this genre (Rich 1979). For a genre that pretends to personal historical veracity, the conflictual interrelatedness of the social world becomes acute and extremely problematic. Moreover, Rich's title succinctly captures the choices involved in the exposition or withholding of the self, and her book of essays amounts to a reconsideration of her self within a personal, political, and academic milieu. This analysis reveals the ideological and aesthetic problems inherent in the process of producing a self-conscious self and, most importantly, the implications of the multiple autobiographical forms that these writers elect as their analogs of self.

In Chapter 4, I turn to the analysis of narrative and examine the work of one of Chicano literature's most prestigious and prolific writers: Rolando Hinojosa. In his Klail City Death Trip Series, he sets forth the life and times of the inhabitants of the fictional Belken County of South Texas. Through the creation of a mythic space, a device somewhat similar to that used by William Faulkner and Gabriel García Márquez, Hinojosa creates a counterworld in which the conflictual social interrelatedness between Mexicans and Anglos can operate in significantly different ways than they do in the real world. He produces a fictional situation of unique empowerment in which the comic plays a major role. By examining revelry, buffo, and the creative dynamics of festival in Hinojosa's writing, I argue that his novels go far beyond the regional picturesque, as some critics have labeled his work, and present a uniquely political point of view. The larger processual dynamics of political activity such as organized protests or acts of heroism give way to small units of social interplay in which language and dialogue dominate. The result is usually a role reversal in which those in power are diminished and those without power are enhanced.

Although Chapter 5 exclusively analyzes poetry, the main emphasis is on the development of a Chicana voice in Chicano literature. I consider the suggestive insights of Julia Kristeva, whose notions about women's time have become influential, and somewhat controversial, in feminist theoretical circles. Taking from her that which might be applicable to Chicana writing, I cross her Eurocentric notions located in psychoanalysis with Chicana theories of borderness. This chapter thus examines the unique processual activity operating in Chicana literature. I address the problematic issues of political struggle that historically have characterized Chicana feminist dialogues (that is, the expectation that Chicanas subordinate their demands for liberation to the struggle for justice for the Chicano people, a position that was advanced by many in the predominantly male-dominated Chicano Movement). Most importantly, I analyze the development of women's time, a movement in which Chicanas become perhaps the most persuasive political component of contemporary Chicano politics. That process of conflict is most clearly akin to Turner's description of persistence and change noted earlier. I further argue that assessing the process of Chicano literary activity in the future clearly reveals that women's time exerts definitive power over the historical moment. Women's time becomes Chicano time—a melding together that promises unique strategies for social and political change.

In the Epilogue I consider the parallel development of Chicano literary theory and discuss some of the possible directions for research. As an aspect of this theoretical consideration, I comment on the pedagogical challenges posed by this literature, not only on its own but also in cross-cultural terms; that is, its place in the development of multicultural theoretical practice. It is in this type of interrogation that we approximate what Edward Said (1983, p. 26) refers to as critical consciousness:

> Criticism in short is always situated; it is skeptical, secular, reflectively open to its own failings. This is by no means to say that it is value-free. Quite the contrary, for the inevitable trajectory of critical consciousness is to arrive at some acute sense of what political, social, and human values are entailed in the reading, production, and transmission of every text. To stand between culture and system is therefore to stand *close to* . . . a concrete reality about which political, moral, and social judgements have to be made and, if not only made, then exposed and demystified.

Similarly, I believe that the future of this literature, as does that of all literatures by people of color in the United States, rests largely on its being effectively introduced into the curricula at all levels, as well as its entrance into the critical consciousness of literary theory. For literature to survive it must be read, and read it we must, for it speaks to the diversity of our constantly shifting constructions of national identity.

Because the story of Chicano literature has no denouement, using prologues and epilogues in a volume of this type seems to belie my purpose. Yet the Epilogue to this collection of essays could also serve as Prologue. These essays reflect the evolution of my own theoretical process and can be seen as the development of a multidimensioned critical perspective affirming that Chicano literature is becoming, that it is processual, and that it is political. I agree with Said's (1983, p. 26) argument that the essay form is particularly appropriate to the type of project undertaken here: "all of what I mean by criticism and critical consciousness is directly reflected not only in the subjects of these essays but in the essay form itself. For if I am to be taken seriously as saying that secular criticism deals with local and worldly situations, and that it is constitutively opposed to the production of massive, hermetic systems, then it must follow that the essay—a comparatively short, investigative, radically skeptical form—is the principal way in which to write criticism." As Said describes his own work, this book's unity is one of "attitude and concern." Subject and form coalesce to expose the praxis of critical consciousness. In this sense, then, these essays are analogs to the literature's continuance.

CHAPTER 1

Time gets lost. You see it
like the spurt of a match in the night, and then it is
suddenly blotted out black under the sun.
            The old people remember yesterday, the women
when their skirts got wet crossing the streams, the men
wood smoke in their hair and sap of piñon trees on their hands.
            But you look up, and where grandfather's guns
used to hang, now books stand, their pages yellowed.
            A dog howls outside
at red evening. The windmill creaks. The mud is fresh
with cow hooves. There is a broken-down bus, and among weeds,
rusty frames of 32s and wooden plow handles, and a grave
or two with paper flowers pink and withered, rain stained.

            In this land there is a graveness, of color
and heart. Here the white sands cannot absorb the rich blood
that sun sponges light from.
            Here wounds open in the heart like cracks
in a mountainside, here there is a solitude in each person,
like a cave where a portion of the person sits and thinks.

            JIMMY SANTIAGO BACA
            "In My Land,"
            from *Immigrants in Our Own Land*

"In Our Own Land"

POLITICS AND CULTURAL

PROCESS IN CONTEMPORARY

CHICANO LITERATURE

The social and political experience of Mexicans in the United States forms the field from which much of what is considered Chicano literature draws its content.[1] This fact, although widely acknowledged, is rarely understood. The above lines from a poem in Jimmy Santiago Baca's *Immigrants in Our Own Land* (1979) point to the complexity of the political and human dimensions of the Mexican's struggle to survive physically and culturally. The elements at war are time and place, and the principals are mutable generations of people in whom is deposited and entrusted the legacy of communal memory, which is threatened by the fragmentation of daily struggle. Baca's perspective is typical of that of much of Chicano literature. Whatever the class or generation, the primary metaphor for the experience is the migrant, who is at once the paradigmatic figure of displacement and oppression and the leading figure of persistence in the vicissitudes of change. As both, the migrant finally underscores life-generating rebellion against cultural erasure.

Arturo Islas (1990b, p. 5) has written eloquently of the importance of understanding the Mexican experience in the United States as that of the migrant as opposed to that of the immigrant:

> Mexicans did not cross an ocean with the intention of starting a brand new life in a "new" world. They were already very much a part of the landscape even before it changed its name from "Mexico" to the "United States" hardly more than a century ago.
>
> These two historical facts are the basis for the migrant concept that I explore in this second novel [*Migrant Souls*] of a trilogy. Migrant psychology, I suggest, is different from immigrant psychology in subtle and significant ways. And it pervades every condition of Mexican people's lives in this country, whether they are citizens or not, from the workers in the fields who harvest the food on our tables to

the students who are asking that the contributions of their culture to North American life be acknowledged in the classroom.

In the United States, the immigrant is not a person but an "alien," a being less than human belonging not to this land and, perhaps, the term implies, not to the human race either. Consequently, the Mexican is asked to feel not only like an immigrant in his or her own land, but like an alien in society as well. The psychological and cultural reaction to this characterization ranges from acquiescence to rebellion. Much of Chicano literature focuses on the rebellion that begins far before the benchmark date of 1848, the close of the Mexican American War, which marked the ceding of over one-third of Mexican territory to the United States. As opposed to the immigrant label, the migrant metaphor positively emphasizes the continuity of experience that informs the movement of peoples in geopolitical and psychosocial spaces in which they claim sovereignty.

The interrelationship between the history of Mexicans residing in the Southwest and the trajectory of the development of the literature must be acknowledged. Ramón Saldívar (1990, p. 5) notes that "for Chicano narrative, *history* is the subtext that we must recover because history itself is the subject of its discourse. History cannot be conceived as mere 'background' or 'context' for this literature; rather, history turns out to be the decisive determinant of the form and content of the literature." This is true of Chicano literature in general. That the region was inhabited by Mexicans and Indians for centuries before the entrance of the Anglo American into this land is vitally significant to understand both the Mexican's tenacious battle to retain cultural as well as political governance and the deep-rootedness of Mexican identity in the territory.

The border between the United States and Mexico did not exist as a legal/political entity until 1924, but the legal designation made little difference to the ever-present migration of Mexican peoples from the interior of Mexico to what had been, prior to the war, the outlying provinces of the Mexican nation. We now refer to this territory as the southwestern United States: the states of Arizona, California, Colorado, New Mexico, and Texas. The movement of Mexican peoples in this locale has taken place over centuries from pre-Columbian to colonial times and persists to the present. Much literature has emerged from and about this migration of peoples. In large measure, the literature has addressed itself to the Anglo American influx into the territory and the political, social, and cultural conflict that ensued. Chicano literature predates the war, in fact, since it chronicles the rising presence of Anglo Americans in the Southwest during the late eighteenth and nineteenth centuries.

The imposition of borders and the creation of attendant political and cultural spaces have fueled a corollary metaphor to that of the migrant. In Gloria Anzaldúa's words (1987, p. 3), "The U.S.-Mexican border *es una herida abierta* where the Third World grates against the first and bleeds. And before a scab forms it hemorrhages again, the lifeblood of two worlds merging to form a third country—a border culture." Guillermo Gómez-Peña (1988, p. 127), performance artist and playwright, comments further:

> My generation, the *chilangos* [slang term for a Mexico City native], who came to "el norte" fleeing the imminent ecological and social catastrophe of Mexico City, gradually integrated itself into otherness, in search of that other Mexico grafted onto the entrails of the et cetera . . . became Chicano-ized. We de-Mexicanized ourselves to Mexi-understand ourselves, some without wanting to, others on purpose. And one day, the border became our house, laboratory, and ministry of culture (or counterculture).

For Anzaldúa and Gómez-Peña, the border metaphorically enlarges the geopolitical space. Yet understanding that space is essential to appreciating the metaphor. In anthropologist Victor Turner's terminology, the Southwest would be the arena in which political, cultural, and social power is contested. Borrowing anthropological terms such as "field" and "arena" allows us to look at the development of Chicano literature as cultural production conditioned by significant events. This perspective also helps distinguish the unique character of the root metaphors and paradigms of experience that have emerged and continue to emerge in this literature.

A discussion of a few basic ideas may help clarify the advantages of wedding the study of anthropology with that of literature. Processual analysis, which Turner uses to advance his study of the Ndembu of Africa, crosses the techniques of cultural and structural functional analysis. Although the intricacies of the method are fascinating, for our purposes the most important aspect of the method is its emphasis on the dynamics of social production. In his forward to *The Ritual Process* (1969, p. vii), Turner writes that "society is a process rather than an abstract system, whether of social structural relations or of symbols and meanings." Moreover, his work develops the idea that the metaphors, symbols, and paradigms generated in these processes transform themselves into distinct, yet interconnected, variations. Isolating and studying processual units, he discovers that they leave "symbolic deposits in social time" (Turner 1974, p. 102). This seeding of symbols exerts definitive force over subsequent cultural production.

Our understanding of the migrant metaphor, and by extension the border, is advanced by studying the field and arenas in which it has developed and has been transformed into new metaphors and incarnations. The value of processual analysis for our purposes lies in its emphasis on transformation connected to social, political, and cultural processes and events. The chapters that follow examine the field and the various arenas of this literature more closely. I begin here by examining Texas-Mexican resistance to Anglo American control of the territory at the end of the nineteenth century because this comprises one of the most well-known arenas of sociopolitical contestation in the field of Mexican/Chicano political and cultural evolution.[2] Turner (1974, p. 17) explains that "'arenas' are the concrete settings in which paradigms become transformed into metaphors and symbols with reference to which political power is mobilized and in which there is a trial of strength between influential paradigm bearers." The conflict between the Anglo American and the Mexican forms just such a space for contestation and for the attendant generation of symbols and metaphors.

The Mexican spirit of rebellion as it emerged in literature was illuminated in the influential study *"With His Pistol in His Hand": A Border Ballad and Its Hero* (1958), in which Américo Paredes recounts the history of the corrido "Gregorio Cortez" and delineates the social and political context for its creation and development. The lengthy chapter on the border, which opens the volume, carefully describes and assesses an area that geographically, as well as politically and culturally, stands as figure and metaphor for the transition between nations and the complex connections that continue to exist for all Mexicans, whether border residents or not. The border is a figure of permanence and change; it has become a metaphor that underscores the dialectical tension between cultures, a tension that forms the core identity of the region and of a people. Paredes's history points to both the political and literary value of this area, which has inspired a tremendous outlay of cultural production, of which the corrido is foremost.

José Limón, in *Mexican Ballads, Chicano Poems* (1992), convincingly argues that the corrido form is precursor to many strains of contemporary Chicano literature. He locates the force of this oral narrative in its embodiment of the contestative properties of social poetry and concludes:

> As a fully active contestative practice in its own right, the epic corrido waned from the 1930s through the 1960s, but

as an active residual practice in new transformed poetic emergences, the epic corrido continued to carry its powerful poetic and counterhegemonic influence into a new period. These transformations played a role in a new social struggle against domination, even as the poetic emergent and residual carried on their own "internal" struggle of poetic influence. This internal struggle in the service of the social requires that the later poets possess a full knowledge of the precursor. The key figure in the transmission of such knowledge is Américo Paredes, the corrido's foremost scholar and foremost poetic son. (Limón 1992, p. 42)

Limón bases much of his argument on Harold Bloom's anxiety of influence theory. By locating his analysis in a clearly patriarchal theoretical model, he draws critical attention to the problematics of a poetic form that encapsulates Mexican patriarchal society. Limón's study significantly advances a critical assessment of the force and influence of the corrido as a male-dominated form and of the patriarchal scholarship that has followed it. He remarks that "as a representation of patriarchy, which it most assuredly is, the corrido necessarily carries within it a large element of internal domination and repression of the gender Other" (Limón 1992, p. 35). Inasmuch as the corrido is significant as a paradigmatic contestative form, arising from historical arenas of conflict, it also illustrates the implied contestation of the female subject, which dominates as the leading arena of contestation in contemporary literature.[3] For these complex reasons and because the corrido is perhaps the literary form most identified with the attitude of resistance to the encroachment of Anglo Americans into the Southwest, it is fitting to begin the following selective review of the literature with this genre.

CONTEST OF THE LAND: AN ORAL LEGACY

The corrido, a narrative song, usually recounts the exploits of a hero who surpasses all odds to prevail against those in power. The hero counters oppression with dignity and honor. In the case of Gregorio Cortez, who was falsely accused of horse stealing and murder, the hero outruns the Texas Rangers in a mad posse chase over half the state. Faced with the pain that his loved ones and community are suffering on his account, according to the legendary story, Cortez eventually allows his own capture. Throughout the numerous variants to this corrido, the requisite elements of the corrido narrative remain: a man who is falsely accused overcomes with cunning and with dignity those considered to be more powerful. Other corridos of this type include "El Corrido de Jacinto Treviño" and "El Corrido de Joaquín Murieta," which recount the deeds of individuals who are now termed "social bandits" because they defended their land and people by confronting the Anglo oppressor (Castillo and Camarillo 1972).

As a literary genre, the corrido has survived, although in somewhat altered form. This transformation is examined more closely in Chapter 2. At this juncture, it is sufficient to note that whereas the classic corrido emerged from an oral tradition, the contemporary corrido, in many instances, has become part of a print tradition. Consequently, the texts of contemporary corridos about modern heroes such as César Chávez, Reies López Tijerina, and John F. Kennedy have been disseminated and published in newspapers and anthologies. Few are now sung accompanied by a guitar, although all can be performed in this manner. Despite changes in its form and content, the corrido has survived because of its power to recall paradigmatic resistance to political and cultural domination. For example, whereas the classic corrido tells the tale of an individual hero, others exalt the image of a collective persona as hero of a community: "El inmigrante," "El ilegal," and "El corrido de la Pensilvania." In these, the migrant becomes the Everyman hero who may not always overpower his oppressors, but whose attitude of resistance helps him to maintain his dignity and independence in threatening situations. The corrido gives form and voice to the Mexican's struggle for survival in oppressive times and in an environment once positive but now sapping and hostile.

The corrido form was precursor to much contemporary Chicano poetry in formal technique as well as in content, and *"With His Pistol in His Hand"* has been instrumental in assessing this relationship. Yet Paredes's examination of the narrative song also led many to see in his work an affirmation of the rich oral legacy of other narrative forms such as the tale, the proverb, and the joke within much of Chicano writing. One of the early collectors and authors of tales, Josephina Niggli (1945), used material that had originated in oral tradition. Her short stories illustrate nineteenth-century courtship styles and recount family feuds that correspond to well-known folktales. Similarly, Daniel Venegas's *Las aventuras de Don Chipote, o cuando los pericos mamen,* originally published in 1928, presents material garnered from a folk tradition. His work has been made available to contemporary audiences through a reprint issued in Mexico City in 1984.

Rudolfo Anaya and José Griego y Maestas published an anthology of old folktales collected from informants in New Mexico. The collection, *Hispanic Folktales of the Southwest: Cuentos Hispanoamericanos* (1980), is presented as a bilingual (Spanish/English) transcription of oral texts. The bilingual mode of publication made the tales accessible to a wider audience and brought them from the oral to the print tradition.

The effects of the sociopolitical turmoil of the region were registered continuously in Mexican folklore on the U.S. side of the border. The shift of the territory from ownership to domination by a foreign people is at the foreground of the notion of the migrant and of the transformation of that figure into a generic metaphor for the change of the Mexican's status in the region. For this reason, many corridos tell of the crossing into the United States and of grueling trips to places like Michigan and California on the migrant route. It is not surprising, then, that Chicano writers have long accepted the migrant as the folk matrix figure for Mexicans in the United States. One of the early writers to focus on the image of the migrant in fiction was José Antonio Villarreal, whose novel *Pocho* (1959) recounts the experiences of Juan and Richard Rubio, father and son. Their lives encompass the physical move from Mexico to the United States and the cultural transformation from Mexican to what Villarreal labels "Pocho" or the cultural hybrid. A number of novels use the migrant as focus for the Mexican experience; among these are Josephina Niggli's *Mexican Village* (1945), Richard Vásquez's *Chicano* (1970), and Raymond Barrio's *The Plum Plum Pickers* (1969). Barrio's work departs from the generational design of the other works by focusing on the cycle of migrant life as it is reflected in the seasons.

CONTEST OF SYMBOLS:
Lo indio y lo chicano

Although migration is a key metaphor discernible throughout the literature written by Mexicans in the United States, during and after the turbulent 1960s the literature explored other symbols and metaphors as well. Certainly the tradition of resistance handed down through the corrido continued with added force. Yet some writers began to look even further back than border events to pre-Columbian Mexico in order to understand the conflicts and contradictions of twentieth-century Chicano life. One writer who based his resistance and social criticism on Mexican history and symbology was Alurista, who published his first one

hundred poems in the collection *Floricanto en Aztlán* in 1971. In it, he drew
on images from Aztec culture and Mayan mythology, juxtaposing them in
jarring relation to the arid, sterile images of what he calls Anglo "Amér-
ika." Alurista uses a mixture of Spanish and English, which further underscores the clash of images within each poem. He is best known for his de-
lineation of a literary aesthetic based on the Indian model of flower and
song, the Aztec philosophy that speaks to the paradox of permanence
within change. Through these explorations into the Mexican cultural past,
Alurista helped define and foster the notion of "Amerindia," which connotes the unification of all Indian peoples into one creative, political, and
social force. His next two collections, *Nationchild Plumaroja* (1972) and *Timespace Huracán* (1976), elaborate upon these ideas.

This type of movement back to pre-Columbian times spawned the
notion of Aztlán, which in Aztec mythology was an undetermined land
north of what is now Mexico. It was the homeland of the Aztecs before
they settled in the Valley of Mexico. For Chicanos, Aztlán symbolized an
ideal state of unification of past and present of a nation divided by war;
Aztlán became the idyll that was lost but could be regained. It was a symbol of hope and an image of natural wholeness from which society had
become estranged. It became a political rallying point and generated an
intense literary activity. The following "Poem in Lieu of Preface" by
Alurista (1970, p. ix) celebrates the fascination and importance of Aztlán:

        it is said

              that MOTECUHZOMA ILHUICAMINA

SENT

                  AN expedition

        looking for the NortherN

               mYthical land

       wherefrom the AZTECS CAME

            la TIERRA

                dE

                      AztláN

         mYthical land for those

         who dream of roses and

swallow thorns

         or for those who swallow thorns

     in powdered milk

feeling guilty about smelling flowers

         about looking for AztláN

Consider the juxtaposition of images: roses and flowers versus thorns and powdered milk. Chicanos are figuratively on that expedition, searching for their natural native homeland; they have been pushed into this journey by the ersatz reality of America, whose powdered milk gags them. They remain intuitively aware that the "northern mythical land" can still be found and still holds the answers to the questions that first compelled Motecuhzoma Ilhuicamina on his search.

Ricardo Sánchez can be considered an antithetical figure to Alurista: his two early collections *Canto y grito mi liberación* (1971) and *Hechizospells* (1976) do not draw on any recent or distant past but rather focus on contemporary images of incarceration, violence, and murder that emerge from an urban, poverty-impacted environment. He does not defer to any preestablished style or symbology. In his tongue-in-cheek "Crítica for an arse poeticus: Coscorones pa'los hocicones y toward a facile universal cogitating (c)academe's tonterías, !ajúa, kahlúa" (Sánchez 1976, p. 313), he makes fun of literary aesthetics in general:

> una flor
> dentro lo rojo
> de un enojo,
>
> panaceas frotando
> the inanity
> de conferencias
> wherein we promenade
> seeking messianic ones
> to charismatically proclaim
> que estos momentos
> son mas
> que los ahuites
> de nuestras vidas comunes[4]

Sánchez is one of many poets whose works scream in outrage at political and social injustice. Among his contemporaries are Abelardo Delgado (*Chicano: 25 Pieces of a Chicano Mind*, 1969) and Sergio Elizondo (*Perros y antiperros*, 1972).

Other poets fall outside the Indianist trend and the social outcry literature, yet their work also affirms Chicano cultural heritage and criticizes society. Among these are Tino Villanueva (*Hay Otra Voz Poems: 1968–1971*, 1972), Ricardo García (*Selected Poetry*, 1973), Juan Gómez-Quiñones (*5th and Grande Vista*, 1974), and Gary Soto (*The Elements of San Joaquín*, 1977; *The Tale* of *Sunlight*, 1978; among others). Alberto Ríos's work (*Whispering to Fool the Wind*, 1982; *The Iguana Killer*, 1985; and *Five Indiscretions*, 1985) also falls into this tradition. These poets use images that are intensely personal, yet they draw larger implications from their idiosyncrasies. Consider the following lines from Gary Soto's poem "History" (1977, p. 41) and note the subtle migrant metaphor that pervades the piece:

> That was the '50s,
> And Grandma in her '50s,
> A face streaked
> From cutting grapes
> And boxing plums.
> I remember her insides
> Were washed of tapeworm,
> Her arms swelled into knobs
> Of small growths—
> Her second son
> Dropped from a ladder
> And was dust.
> And yet I do not know
> The sorrows
> That sent her praying
> In the dark of a closet,
> The tear that fell
> At night
> When she touched
> Loose skin
> Of belly and breasts.
> I do not know why
> Her face shines
> Or what goes beyond this shine,
> Only the stories
> That pulled her
> From Taxco to San Joaquin,
> Delano to Westside,
> The places
> In which we all begin.

For Soto, those "stories" are the connections between himself, his grandmother, and his people, although his relationship to the stories, which are "the places in which we all begin," is vague: "I do not know."

This lack of clarity implies and underscores a paradox; the link with a communal past is locked within the minutiae of individual experience. Gone are the heroes of border corridos or even the Everyman hero of migrant songs. Gone is their testimony of lived experience. Enter the Chicano with a precarious grasp of a fading past and a self-conscious need to recall origins, no matter how dim, and affirm contests, no matter how obscure.

Within this type of response to experience, the autobiography emerges in Chicano literature. Ernesto Galarza's *Barrio Boy* (1971) is a good example. It chronicles the complexities of assimilation, the need of a young man to connect himself with a cultural past and yet fit into an alien future. Here the individual confronts the cultural locus in order to refashion a functional logos in Anglo American society. With vastly different results, Richard Rodriguez's *Hunger of Memory* (1983), the focus of Chapter 3, is a similar attempt. In his autobiography, Rodriguez sheds any Mexican cultural referent, whether it be language or family, in order for the new self, the public "Rich-heard Road-ree-guess," to operate successfully in the Anglo American world.

Oscar Zeta Acosta's *Autobiography of a Brown Buffalo* (1974) takes a different stance; it emerges from a tradition in which political satire becomes the impetus and mode for the presentation. Acosta's work is more a commentary or editorial statement on the Chicano Movement of the sixties and less an account of the subjective nuances of character transformation. Cherríe Moraga's *Loving in the War Years: Lo que nunca pasó por sus labios* (1983) expands the genre in form and style with her lesbian feminist perspective. During the 1960s and 1970s, the literary output and publications of Chicano writers increased dramatically. Only a few of the more widely known poets and autobiographers whose work has influenced those who followed are mentioned here.

The novel form also benefited from the increased literary activity of the period. The publication house Quinto Sol perhaps carries the greatest responsibility for publishing the work of Chicano novelists very early. Through its national competitions and literary prizes, this editorial house was at the forefront of Chicano fiction. The literary prize winners include Tomás Rivera for *Y no se lo tragó la tierra: And the Earth Did Not Part* (1971), Rudolfo Anaya for *Bless Me, Ultima* (1972), and Rolando Hinojosa-Smith for *Estampas del valle y otras obras: Sketches of the Valley and Other Works* (1973). All of these have become classic works and are taught in many Chicano literature courses. Three of these novelists continued to write and to evolve as writers. Rudolfo Anaya subsequently published the novels *Heart of Aztlán*

(1976), *Tortuga* (1979), and *Albuquerque* (1992) and edited several collections of short stories. Tomás Rivera added essays on Chicano literature to his achievement in fiction before his untimely death in 1984. His novel is often considered perhaps the best work of Chicano fiction of this period.

Rolando Hinojosa continues to write and publish prolifically. Most of his novels form the Klail City Death Trip Series, in which he chronicles the genealogical and political history of the fictional Belken County in South Texas. His recent publications include *Klail City y sus alrededores* (winner of the Casa de las Américas Prize for Literature, Cuba, 1976), *Mi querido Rafa* (1981), *The Valley* (1983), and *Korean Love Songs* (1978), a collection of narrative poems. In 1985 he released two new books: *Dear Rafe* (English translation of *Mi querido Rafa*), an epistolary novel that sets forth the correspondence between the cornerstone protagonists of the series, Jehú Malacara and Rafe Buenrostro, and *Partners in Crime*, a detective novel featuring Rafe as the investigator. *Claros varones de Belken: Fair Gentlemen of Belken County* was released in 1986, *Becky and Her Friends* in 1989, and *Useless Servants* in 1993.

Hinojosa's literary output and influence in Chicano letters are immense, and his Belken County is an analog to the arena of contestation so central to the development of this literature. His work demands closer scrutiny, and I emphasize the comic, one of the unique elements that characterize much of his writing, in Chapter 4. Through the comic, Hinojosa manifests the resistance to Anglo American rule that forms such a large part of Texas-Mexican consciousness and of the sensibilities of the Chicano in general.

Another writer not published by Quinto Sol but of great significance is Ron Arias, whose *Road to Tamazunchale* (1975, reprinted 1987) is a staple of Chicano literature courses. Arturo Islas's *The Rain God: A Desert Tale* (1985) and *Migrant Souls* (1990), a deep and humanistic psychological portrayal of a Mexican family in El Paso, move Chicano literature firmly into the twentieth century.

The 1970s also produced a canon of literature in Spanish. The works of Tomás Rivera and the early novels of Rolando Hinojosa were originally written in Spanish, although they were printed in bilingual formats. Two other novelists, Alejandro Morales, *Caras viejas y vino nuevo* (1975), and Miguel Méndez, *Peregrinos de Aztlán* (1975), also published works in Spanish. Méndez's text includes Yaqui phrases along with the Spanish in a bold style that masterfully evokes dialogue. Both novels contribute significantly to the canon of Chicano literature, but because they are in Spanish they are rarely taught in Chicano literature classes offered through English departments.

Literary activity was generated in other genres as well, particularly in drama. Perhaps the best-known Chicano playwright is Luis Valdez, whose *Actos* (1971) is one of the major contributions to the field. Valdez experimented with guerrilla theater as well as with modern production techniques. The most widely known result was *Zoot Suit,* a mixture of music and historical commentary. A play of tremendous vitality, it achieved great success in Los Angeles. Carlos Morton collected his own plays in *The Many Deaths of Danny Rosales and Other Plays* (1983). Estela Portillo-Trambley moved from prose to drama in *Sor Juana and Other Plays* (1983), as did Cherríe Moraga in *Giving Up the Ghost* (1986).

The essay, a genre rarely addressed by critics, is garnering increased attention in Chicano literature. From Octavio Romano's "Goodbye Revolution—Hello Slum" in the late 1960s to Juan Gómez-Quiñones's *On Culture* (1977), the emphasis on argument and style can be traced to the tradition of great Latin American writers. Authors such as José E. Limón, "Stereotyping and Chicano Resistance: An Historical Dimension" (1973), and Arturo Madrid-Barela, "In Search of the Authentic Pachuco" (1973), fall within this tradition as well.

Women writers have also contributed continually and significantly to the development of Chicano literature, and their voice is perhaps the most important element directing the development of the literature in the 1980s and 1990s. Among the early writers of fiction are Josephina Niggli, *Mexican Village* (1945) and Estela Portillo-Trambley, *Rain of Scorpions* (1975), as well as the poets Lucha Corpi, *Palabras de mediodía: Noon Words* (1980), Bernice Zamora, *Restless Serpents* (1976), Angela de Hoyos, *Arise, Chicano! and Other Poems* (1975), Lorna Dee Cervantes, *Emplumada* (1981), and Margarita Cota-Cárdenas, *Noches despertando inconciencias* (1977).

Just as the publishing house Quinto Sol played a major role in the dissemination of Chicano literature during the early 1970s, the 1980s saw a similar boost to literary production. Arte Público Press actively began to seek manuscripts and not only published the works but gave exposure to the writers as well. In the mid-1980s Arte Público Press began publishing the following women writers: Pat Mora, *Chants* (1984), *Borders* (1986), and *Communion* (1991); Ana Castillo, *Women Are Not Roses* (1984); Helena Viramontes, *The Moths* (1990); Evangelina Vigil, *Thirty an' Seen a Lot* (1985) as well as the anthology *Woman of Her Word* (1984); Denise Chávez, *The Last of the Menu Girls* (1986); and Sandra Cisneros, *The House on Mango Street* (1983), which received the National Book Award.

Women have published in other presses as well. *Curandera,* a collection of poems by Carmen Tafolla, was produced by M & A Editions in 1983.

Cherríe Moraga and Gloria Anzaldúa edited *This Bridge Called My Back* (1981), a collection of poems and essays published by Persephone Press; and Sandra Cisneros's *Woman Hollering Creek* was published by Random House in 1991. Poetry, narrative, and criticism have been collected in *Third Woman: Texas and More* (1986), a volume edited by Norma Alarcón.

The impact that women's writing is having on Chicano literary circles is only beginning to be felt. In the past, both male and female writers addressed themselves largely to the problematics of place as they undertook the complex task of unfolding the Chicano experience. Hinojosa's characters live out their existence in the fictional Belken County in the South Texas Lower Río Grande Valley, struggling constantly with the opposing force of the Anglo American presence. Tomás Rivera explores the psychological and political dilemmas of migrant life, the movement from place to place, and its effects on family, religious belief, and sense of self. Chicanas are directing their critical eye to another dimension of the experience: time. Their social commentary is beginning to redefine the historical moment as one no longer tied to place or event, such as the Mexican American War, nor to precursors like the Aztecs, but rather to the historical moment as it is connected to gender relations.

As women's voices begin to be heard, the political and social struggle must alter to accommodate their view. Women's literature gives renewed force to Chicano/a (the term preferred by most Chicana feminists) literature and begins to direct a vital dialogue within Chicano politics as well. In Chapter 5, I argue that Chicana literature marks a qualitative change in the root metaphor that provided the context for the development of the literature. Women writers are challenging the male-dominated form of the corrido by asserting the female logos as the center of communal resistance, survival, continuity, and, most importantly, political strength. Their voice transforms the dimensions of sociopolitical consciousness and, by extension, the processes of literary activity itself.

Consider the following title poem from Lorna Dee Cervantes's *Emplumada* (1981, p. 66), with its images of loss, gain, and freedom. Her verse suggests the direction in which women writers are now leading:

> When summer ended
> the leaves of snapdragons withered
> taking their shrill-colored mouths with them.
> They were still, so quiet. They were
> violet where umber now is. She hated
> and she hated to see
> them go. Flowers

born when the weather was good—this
she thinks of, watching the branch of peaches
daring their ways above the fence, and further,
two hummingbirds, hovering, stuck to each other,
arcing their bodies in grim determination
to find what is good, what is
given them to find. These are warriors

distancing themselves from history.
They find peace
in the way they contain the wind
and are gone.

As Cervantes indicates, like the hummingbirds who "in grim determination" search "to find what is good, what is / given them to find," the
struggle is altered; the stakes are transformed. The battle has different dimensions; it is not a history based on chronology, but a dialectic of con-
tainment and movement, a free flight in which history itself is redefined.

CHICANO CRITICAL RESPONSE

The growing canon of criticism marks the development
of the literature as a subject for its own scrutiny. The major early statements emerge from the discipline of folklore. Américo Paredes's "With His
Pistol in His Hand" (1958) and "Some Aspects of Folk Poetry" (1964) turned
many young scholars toward the rich legacy of oral culture that characterized and continues to influence Mexican literary output. Later Paredes's
article "The Folk Base of Chicano Literature," along with Joseph Sommers's "Critical Approaches to Chicano Literature," formed the cornerstone of what continues to be one of the most important critical volumes
available on the literature: Modern Chicano Writers (1979), edited by Joseph
Sommers and Tomás Ybarra-Frausto. The collection also includes specific
critical analyses of several influential authors, including Alurista and
Tomás Rivera. This collection of essays traces its theoretical origins to
folklore studies as well as to anthropology, literature, and politics. It seeks
to understand the trajectory of the literature out of the social, political,
and cultural life of Mexicans in the United States and is a pioneering work
of the critics who, early on, advanced the process of criticism of Chicano
literature.

Two other collections stand out because they reflect the critical focus of
the 1970s and 1980s: The Identification and Analysis of Chicano Literature (1979),

edited by Francisco Jiménez, and *A Decade of Chicano Literature* (1982), edited by Luis Leal and others. An important volume edited by María Herrera-Sobek and Helena María Viramontes, *Chicana Creativity and Criticism: Charting New Frontiers in American Literature,* was published in 1988. During these two decades, numerous articles appeared in literary periodicals such as *El Grito* (Berkeley), *Maíze* (San Diego), *Metamórfosis* (Seattle), *MELUS* (Los Angeles and Cincinnati), the *Revista Chicano-Riqueña* (Houston), *Caracol* (San Antonio), *De Colores* (New Mexico), and *Aztlán: International Journal of Chicano Studies Research* (Los Angeles), to name only a few. Much of the early critical work appeared in these periodicals, whose importance to the development and study of the literature should not be underestimated. Unfortunately, considering the problems associated with academic publishing in general and with alternative publishing in particular, the longevity of these journals is a troublesome issue.

The 1980s produced several important genre studies as well: Juan Bruce-Novoa's *Chicano Poetry: A Response to Chaos* (1982) and Marta Sánchez's *Contemporary Chicana Poetry: An Approach to an Emerging Literature* (1985), among others. Bruce-Novoa, following the Latin American lead in using the form of authorial interview as criticism, published *Chicano Authors: Inquiry by Interview* (1980). Jorge Huerta's *Chicano Theater: Themes and Forms* (1982) is one of the leading statements in the field of drama.

In addition to these studies, several journals also issued special volumes on the literature. *El Grito* is perhaps the leading example of this type of publication. *Aztlán: International Journal of Chicano Studies Research* dedicated a double volume to "Mexican Folklore and Folk Art in the United States" in 1982, and the *Revista Chicano-Riqueña* released a memorial volume on Tomás Rivera in 1985. The first comprehensive study of Rolando Hinojosa's narrative, *The Rolando Hinojosa Reader: Essays Historical and Critical* (1985), edited by José David Saldívar, is a valuable guide. In recent years a number of books on Chicano literature and theory have been published, including Ramón Saldívar's *Chicano Narrative: The Dialectics of Difference* (1990), José David Saldívar's *Dialectics of Our America: Genealogy, Cultural Critique, and Literary History* (1991), and José David Saldívar and Héctor Calderón, eds., *Criticism in the Borderlands: Studies in Chicano Literature, Culture, and Ideology* (1991).

In all, the critical response continues to grow and reflect the importance of this literature within the American literary canon, as well as within an international context. In many ways, the linguistic, cultural, and literary complexity of the literature demands critical responses that go beyond disciplinary boundaries and perhaps reside most comfortably in a comparative literature perspective.

CONCLUSION

The social, political, and cultural conflict that forms the context for the development of Chicano literature has not abated. The arenas in which power is assessed and contested may vary, but issues of political and cultural usurpation remain at the center of Chicano art. Juan Gómez-Quiñones (1977, p. 20) observes that "the forms and ethos of one art must be broken—the art of domination; another art must be rescued and fashioned—the art of resistance. For the latter, the aesthetic ethos is the result of sensibility developed through experience, identification, and critical intelligence. This art emerges from the experience of struggle." Conflict thus informs the practice of Chicano literary production. How and why and to what extent the process has been and continues to be defined by the agonistic dimensions of Chicano life is the subject of the following chapters.

CHAPTER 2

The performance transforms itself. . . .
Traditional framings may have to be reframed—
new bottles made for new wine.

VICTOR TURNER
"Social Dramas and Stories about Them"

Chicano Poetry
and the Political Age

THE CANALES / CÓRDOVA

CORRIDOS AS SOCIAL DRAMA

On January 29, 1973, the following account appeared in the community newspaper *El Grito del Norte* from Española, New Mexico (p. 4):

> A year ago at midnight, on top of a desolate mesa just outside Albuquerque, Antonio Córdova and Rito Canales were gunned down by a group of six New Mexico police. Nine or ten bullets were pumped into Antonio while six bullets were fired into Rito's body, mostly his back. Although police claimed they had caught the two 29 year old Chicanos trying to steal dynamite, few of our people were convinced by the police explanation of events and almost none believed that such terrible force was really needed to stop them. People knew that both Antonio and Rito worked with Las Gorras Negras [The Black Berets], a Chicano community organization, and had recently been collecting information on state prison conditions (Rito was an ex-pinto) and police brutality. Antonio had also worked with *El Grito* as a reporter and photographer until shortly before he died.
>
> The killings of Jan. 29 have never been forgotten, although no state or federal agency took any action for justice. Attorney General David Norvell white-washed the police in his so-called report. The U.S. Civil Rights Commission promised action but . . .
>
> On Jan. 24, 1973, María Córdova—mother of Antonio—filed a suit for $300,000 damages in Albuquerque District Court against the six police.

This article and the action taken by María Córdova followed a year of intensive newspaper coverage of the events of January 29, 1972. The newspaper printed not only feature-length articles and biographies of the victims, but also excerpts from the Norvell Report; testaments about the men's value to the community appeared in a segment entitled "Unheard Voices of the Families." In addition, letters by well-known Raza leaders throughout the nation were published in the section "Raza Speaks Out on the Murders." Interspersed through these segments were numerous corridos and poems about the January 29 alleged murders, which were signed by family members of the slain men (María Córdova, the mother, and Carlos Córdova, the brother) as well as interested friends and political supporters, including a poem by José Antonio Soler del Valle, from Puerto Rico.

In conjunction with the news reports and editorial commentary, the poems constitute an important aspect of the rhetorical presentation of the event during the year preceding, and almost a year following, María Córdova's filing of the lawsuit. This configuration of reportage, corrido, and poem suggests important questions about the development of Chicano poetry during the years 1965–1975, a period which roughly corresponds to the public activist stage of the Chicano Movement and which poses issues of interest in understanding the evolution of poetry in what some refer to as the Postmovement era. Since chronological divisions of social activity, such as these, are central to this discussion of the parameters of the social drama, these issues are discussed later.

Let me begin the discussion with consideration of the essay "The Folk Base of Chicano Literature," published in 1964 and reprinted in 1979, in which Américo Paredes delineates an ideological framework under which most critics of Chicano literature implicitly have operated since. In it he posits the notion of two Mexicos, *Méjico de adentro* (inside Mexico)—all that is encompassed within the territorial boundaries of the Republic of Mexico—and *Méjico de afuera* (outside Mexico)—all those Mexicans (whether Mexican nationals or not) who remain outside. By noting the two categories, he attests not only to differences between the two groups, but to linkages as well. His perspective gives us an understanding of the Mexican American as a separate subject who is linked to, and yet opposed to, both Mexican and Anglo American cultures. Of greatest concern here is his assertion (Paredes 1979, p. 10) that "the Mexican saw himself and all that he stood for as continually challenging a foreign people who treated him, for the most part, with disdain. Being Mexican meant remaining inviolable in the face of overwhelming attack on one's personality. Under these circumstances, for a Mexican to accept North American values was to desert under fire."

Although Paredes's comments refer to a particular era (the period immediately preceding and following the Mexican American War), his ideas remain germane to the Mexican experience that followed. He implicitly argues the existence of the Other, the foreign power, the enemy who threatens the continuity and survival of a people's cultural and psychological integrity. In the time about which Paredes writes, the Other was the Anglo American and, in particular, his/her institutional representative, the rinche (Texas Ranger); later on, the Other became the Anglo American dominant authority, either the police or the amorphous *they* of the hegemony under which contemporary Mexicans felt themselves to be living.

According to Paredes, it is in folklore that the Mexican finds and retains an identity. He clearly posits this idea in his essay "Folklore, lo Mexicano, and Proverbs," reprinted in 1982 (p. 1): "In other words, folklore is of particular importance to minority groups such as the Mexican Americans because their basic sense of identity is expressed in a language with an 'unofficial' status, different from the one used by the official culture. We can say, then, that while in Mexico the Mexican may well seek lo mexicano in art, literature, philosophy, or history—as well as in folklore—the Mexican American would do well to seek his identity in his folklore."

For Paredes the corrido, because it was a folk-determined genre, was uniquely suited to present the interethnic conflict of the period. And as we can see in *El Grito del Norte*, the corrido continues to be similarly used. The differences between the classic corrido dealing with border conflict and the contemporary corrido (as represented by the Canales/Córdova one discussed in this chapter) are technical, structural, and, as we shall see, functional as well. By examining the divergence between the two, we also see similarities and, in doing so, more closely approximate and understand what Paredes ideologically posited as the folk base of Chicano literature. That Chicano literature proceeds out of a folk base has been a common assumption of most Chicano critics. That it evolves out of an oral tradition is a widely held corollary to this belief. The implications of these notions for the conceptualization of Chicano literary criticism are my concern in this chapter. Since folk base does not necessarily carry the verbal connotations of orality, it would be beneficial, I believe, to examine these critical assumptions more closely through an investigation of the folksong or the corrido, which has become, as I have argued in Chapter 1, the emblematic form of Chicano literary activity.

In his 1964 essay "Some Aspects of Folk Poetry," Paredes isolates three important elements of folksong: (1) a binary structure producing balance and contrast, (2) conventional language and use of formula, and (3) performance. The first two points need not be discussed here since they have been addressed at length by others, particularly by Manuel Peña in his

"Folksong and Social Change: Two Corridos as Interpretive Sources" (1982, pp. 13–38; see also Peña 1985). I focus on the third aspect, performance, since most Chicano critics have interpreted Paredes's notion of the folk base of Chicano literature to refer to its origins in oral forms.

Paredes (1964) tells us that three factors must be taken into consideration when discussing performance: (1) the influence of chant or song on both rhythm and diction; (2) the context in which a folk poem is performed, and (3) the performer as an actor, a personality. In analyzing the corridos produced in reaction to the Canales/Córdova situation, the second and third points are most useful. Paredes (1964, p. 217) is clearly correct in his assessment that "when folk poetry is written down . . . the repetitions, the refrains, the strong parallelistic devices that hold it together may become too monotonous to an ear that is guided by the eye." Thus, the Canales/Córdova corridos perhaps lack the felicity of song and may strike us with their questionable diction. They do, however, present an innovation in the notion of context and performance. While Paredes focuses on the contextual relationship of the corrido to the politico-historical milieu, as well as to the event of its performance, he emphasizes the individual folk performer. I argue that in these corridos a more encompassing type of performance is evident—one that emphasizes the notion of the actor and that more closely approaches Victor Turner's notion of the social drama.

In *Dramas, Fields, and Metaphors: Symbolic Action in Human Society*, Turner presents the major tenets of his theory concerning the processual nature of human activity and defines in more detail these "structures of experience" that he considers to be fundamental units of human action. In "Social Dramas and Stories about Them" he explains the "species of 'element of the historical field' or 'event,' . . . which is cross-culturally isolable and which exhibits, if it is allowed to come to full term, a characteristic processual structure, a structure that holds firm whether one is considering a macro- or micro-historical event of this type"; he then argues that this unit, the social drama, is "the social ground of many types of narrative" (Turner 1981, p. 141). Furthermore, he clarifies: "I tend to regard the social drama in its full formal development, its full phase structure, as a process of converting particular values and ends, distributed over a range of actors, into a system (which is always temporary and provisional) of shared and consensual meaning" (Turner 1981, p. 152).

The elements of *event, narrativity,* and *shared consensual meaning* are fundamental to the social drama. Moreover, reflexivity attends all these elements since social dramas constitute "ways in which a group tries to scrutinize, portray, understand, and then act upon itself" (Turner 1981, p. 152). These activities, Turner argues, are processual; that is, they contain a structure that roughly conforms to four phases: breach, crisis, redress, and either re-integration or recognition of schism. And these phases "occur within groups of persons who share values and interests and who have a real or al-leged common history" (Turner 1981, p. 152).

A cursory look shows that Mexican history easily lends itself to the so-cial drama interpretation. Turner acknowledges this fact in his extensive study of Miguel Hidalgo y Costilla and his role in the struggle for Mexi-can independence. José Limón, in *Mexican Ballads, Chicano Epic: History, Social Dramas, and Poetic Persuasions* (1986), argues the benefits of using social drama to interpret Chicano political events by focusing on two periods of what he calls greater Mexican history: 1890–1930 and 1966–1972. He bases this periodization on Turner's requisites for a politically keyed conflict sit-uation, which include certain dramatistic elements that play out a story or analog to ordered experience. Of primary importance to Limón's formula-tion is Turner's third phase of the social drama, redressive action: "It is in the redressive phase that both pragmatic techniques and symbolic action reach their fullest expression. For the society, group, community, associa-tion, or whatever may be the social unit, is here at its most 'self-conscious' and may attain the clarity of someone fighting in a corner for his life" (Turner 1974, p. 41).

The key elements in this passage are "pragmatic techniques and sym-bolic action," which Limón (1986a, p. 2) perceives to be essential to un-derstanding the two periods of Mexican/Chicano social drama that he isolates:

> The first social drama I have in mind is the dualistic inter-national "disharmonic" social process that, on the Mexi-can side of the border, reaches its utmost clarity in the extended event we call the Mexican Revolution of 1910, and, on this side of the border, although with less clarity, consists of an extended radical questioning of Anglo-American political authority, particularly in Texas. . . .
> The second social drama emerges between 1966 and 1972 and also consists in part of a radical Mexican-American political critique of Anglo-American authority although encompassing an extended Southwestern regional zone.

In this schema of the Mexican/Chicano social drama, Limón argues that the corrido becomes a significant form of symbolic redressive action. His assertion is well grounded in the generative nature of the social drama, which Turner (1981, p. 154) clarifies: "The social drama, then, I regard as the experiential matrix from which the many genres of cultural performance, beginning with redressive ritual and juridical procedures and eventually including oral and literary narrative, have been generated." Taking his cue from Turner, Limón understands the corrido to be not only a form of redressive symbolic action but also a form in transformation, that is, one that bridges his periodization of the Mexican/Chicano social drama and that becomes a key element in the residual effects of the drama still being played out in Anglo/Chicano conflicts arising in the Southwest today.[1]

It is not necessary to recount all of Limón's useful argument here, but it is important to reaffirm his analysis of the corrido as a symbolic form, which changes and is transformed by the particular events that compose his two periods of social drama. Turner (1974, p. 43) lays the groundwork for this notion of the transformation of symbolic forms: "I would point out too that at the linguistic level of 'parole,' each phase has its own speech forms and styles, its own rhetoric, its own kinds of nonverbal languages and symbolisms . . . [and] that there will be certain important generic affinities between the speeches and languages of the crisis phase everywhere, of the redressive phase everywhere, of the restoration of peace everywhere." He adds: "Cultural performances may be viewed as 'dialectical dancing partners' . . . of the perennial social drama to which they give meaning appropriate to the specificities of time, place and culture" (Turner 1981, p. 155).

We can infer from Turner's analysis that this proliferation of expressive forms takes place in time, demonstrates a temporal structure, and, as such, is subject to change. The textuality of the social drama, then, can only be understood by keeping these temporal dimensions in mind. Frank Lentricchia understands this textuality when he reconsiders Raymond Williams's thoughts on the issue of hegemony. His analysis is instructive for this discussion. Lentricchia (1983, p. 15) reminds us that hegemony too "is a process that 'has continually to be renewed, recreated, defended, and modified' because it is continually being 'resisted, limited, altered, challenged by pressures not at all its own.' This is to say that hegemony is 'never either total or exclusive' and that it is best understood dramatically—I mean agonistically. . . ." His comments are germane considering that Mexican history has been characterized by hegemonic conflict. Paredes has formulated this history in terms of the antagonistic Other, Turner has characterized it as social drama, and Limón has postulated it as social drama attended by symbolic action in the services of transformation.

If we use Limón's schema, Gregorio Cortez is a figure who is associated with the first period of the Mexican/Chicano social drama and who reflects his community in his resistance, an attitude incarnated in his celebrated flight from a posse across Texas. But most importantly he is the subject of one of the most well-known corridos of the time. Less than one hundred years later, Antonio Córdova and Rito Canales also resisted what they perceived to be their unjust domination by the Anglo American and were murdered for their efforts. They too became the subject of corridos, but the circumstances of the production and presentation of this symbolic form differ significantly from those that chronicled Cortez's exploits. Whereas the "Corrido de Gregorio Cortez" was performed by numerous folk artists across the Southwest, in small groups and large, the mode of communication was primarily oral. For the chroniclers of the Canales/Córdova situation, the poem operates in concert with significantly different actants; the report, the biography, and the epistle replace the figures surrounding the campfire.

The process of transforming symbolic forms that Limón discusses is evident here. The political and cultural nature of the activities that produced both of these symbolic forms connects them. They emerge from different historical moments in the social drama, but their essential political nature remains, if political means action associated with struggle. Turner confirms the political element in the social drama when he observes that social dramas are in large measure political. He means that they arise out of crisis and function to redress a social breach. Moreover, "there is an interdependent, perhaps dialectic, relationship between social dramas and genres of cultural performance" (Turner 1981, p. 149).

In both cases (Cortez and Canales/Córdova) the corrido is a genre of cultural performance that acts dialectically within the larger social drama. The link, then, between the corrido and the social drama does not lie in orality per se, but in narrativity itself, in the politically laden event upon which the narrative is based, and, most importantly, in the social group from which it springs, whose constant crises revolve around the dysfunction or breach produced by the Anglo American Other. These elements are the paradigmatic dimensions of the saga of Mexican/Chicano resistance to domination; this is the root metaphor from which others are born. Turner's (1981, p. 149) observation, then, that the story feeds "back into the social process, providing it with a rhetoric, a mode of emplotment, and a meaning," seems to hold true. Moreover, these genres of cultural performance that attend the drama or story also appear to function as "our native way of manifesting ourselves to ourselves and of declaring where power and meaning lie and how they are distributed" (Turner 1981, p. 154).

Cultural performances are time bound: they provide meaning by positing a past and a history, which draws attention to these forms as reactions to, recorders of, and producers of social change. Turner (1981, p. 156) tells us that "the performance transforms itself. True, as I said, the rules may frame the performance, but the flow of action and interaction within that frame may conduce to hitherto unprecedented insights and even generate new symbols and meanings, which may be incorporated into subsequent performances. Traditional framings may have to be reframed—new bottles made for new wine."

I suggest that the corrido is reframed in the context of a type of social drama performance that is defined within the rhetorical boundaries of, in this case, the newspaper. Other reframings are possible and do occur, such as the corridos generated in the Delano-strike picket lines or included in memorial documents for dead leaders (see *Raíz fuerte que no se arranca* 1983). Yet two essential elements, which confirm the political functionality, always remain: (1) the overt and implied Other and (2) the emphasis on event, or narrativity, to transform that event into larger social action.

Let me begin discussing the rhetorical presentation of the Canales/ Córdova slayings in *El Grito del Norte* by first considering the following corrido by María Córdova, which was published in that newspaper on May 19, 1972:

UNA POEMA POR LA MADRE DE ANTONIO

Voy a escribir unas linias
de lo que hace poco pasó
Mataron a Antonio y Rito
en Albuquerque Nuevo Mexico

Mil novecientos setenta y dos
El viente y nueve de enero
Mataron a Antonio y Rito
pero hicieron sus planes primero

Callaron en Manos de hombres
de duro Corazón
los Mataron en Black Mesa
sin ninguna compasión

Seis tiros le dieron a Rito
a Antonio le dieron diez

ellos querian estar seguros
que no se levantaron otra vez

Los sacaron a Black Mesa
los Mataron a traición
para que ellos no pudieron
aparecer en el programa de la televisión

Toda la gente sabe
que los mataron en sangre fria
el crimen que les levantaron
no lo han podido probar todavía

El dia viente y ocho de enero
hicieron todos sus planes
para cometer este crimen
y quedar ellos libres de sus afanes

Estos eran dos hombres
que no temian morir
pusieron sus vidas en peligro
porque no querian ver a su Pueblo sufrir

Dos hombres que los mataron
eran seis hombres inhumanos
pero la sangre que se derramieron
será requirida de sus manos

Habia doscientos personas
que demandaron la Verdad
pero ellos estaban dentro de cuatro poderes
cubiertos con la capa de la autoridad

Antonio no nesesitaba dinamita
para defender sus derechos
tenía pluma, papel y su camara
para proverles sus hechos

Ellos no saben que un dia
que al juicio tendran que pasar
y allí delante de un juez justo,
no se podrán escapar

Vimos el retrato de Anita
con su pequeño niñito

Y nos parte el corazon
porque su padre no pudo ver a su hijito

No soy poeta ni soy nada
solo soy una madre de un hijo querido
y hoy mismo me encuentro
con mi corazon herido

Ya con este me despido
teniendo mucho más que decir
y esperando que la Raza Nuestra
En lo futuro se sepa unir.[2]

The author of the poem has observed some of the conventions of the corrido form.[3] She retells the event with attention to date and place: "Mil novecientos setenta y dos / El viente y nueve de enero / Mataron a Antonio y Rito / pero hicieron sus planes primero" (Nineteen hundred and seventy-two / the twenty-ninth of January / They killed Antonio and Rito / but they made their plans beforehand). From here she leads us through the details of the story—where and how they were killed: "Callaron en Manos de hombres / de duro Corazón / los Mataron en Black Mesa / sin ninguna compasión" (They fell into the hands of men / with hard hearts / who killed them at Black Mesa / without any compassion). And "Seis tiros le dieron a Rito / a Antonio le dieron diez / ellos querian estar seguros / que no se levantaron otra vez" (They shot Rito six times / they shot Antonio ten / they wanted to make sure / they would never get up again). The action moves from the actual murder to the official investigation of the crime, and the speaker makes another contextual shift: "Estos eran dos hombres / que no temian morir / pusieron sus vidas en peligro / porque no querian ver a su Pueblo sufrir" (These were two men / who did not fear death / they put their lives in danger / because they didn't want to see their people suffer). The speaker solidifies the communal identification of the victims: "Antonio no nesesitaba dinamita / para defender sus derechos / tenía pluma, papel y su camara / para proverles sus hechos" (Antonio did not need dynamite / to defend his rights / He had pen, paper, and his camera / to prove his deeds).

Obviously the allusion is to the repeated formula from the border corrido about Gregorio Cortez, who "defendió su derecho con su pistola en la mano" (defended his rights with his pistol in his hand). The acts of resistance of one cultural hero are superimposed on those of the intellectual warrior who uses a pen and not a pistol in his fight. The play against the oral corrido subtext is placed in the foreground here. Moreover, as in the classic corrido form, María Córdova ends with the formulaic despedida or farewell: "No soy poeta ni soy nada" (I am not a poet, I am not anything) and "Ya con este me despido / teniendo mucho más que decir / y esperando que la Raza Nuestra / En lo futuro se sepa unir" (With this I say farewell / having so much more to say / and hoping that our beloved people / in the future will know how to unite).

The shift from recounting the event to showing the position of the victim within the Chicano community serves several purposes. It allows the speaker to deliver the underlying message of the poem: it is not Antonio who has the power to effect change, but his fellow community, who must unite, become powerful, and produce change. The event—the murder of the two men—serves a larger meaning and purpose: the unification of the community against the Other. Most importantly, the murders and the form in which they are explained to the community (that is, the corrido) comprise part of a historical and cultural drama that has been taking place since Anglo Americans encroached on the Southwest. The deaths of these leaders of the Chicano movement form a part of the text of conflict and resistance that continues to be played out in Southwest history.

Clearly, the Canales/Córdova manifestation is significantly different from the classic ballads of the border. The rhetorical function of the corrido as it had been sung in small communal settings in the ranchos or at family celebrations gives way to a much wider rhetorical situation like the one I am investigating here. The nature of the teller and the listener has changed radically. The interaction between the single folk performer and the audience has widened considerably. Now the reactions to the drama are expressed through printed letters, poems, testimonies, and news reports. We see in El Grito del Norte a tableau effect in which each element in the presentation plays off against another to produce a simulated "teller/ listener" relationship. The direct address of the corrido provides the core situation, to which the rest of the elements in the tableau react and provide consensual response. The series of newspaper tableaux (in the case of the Canales/Córdova situation, the presentation of the event continues through several editions of the newspaper and spans several years) expresses the idea of crisis and the need for redress. As I have noted, the corrido itself carries the dynamics of an event, a narrativity, and a call to action based on a consensus of values, all essential elements of the social drama. As such, it plays a crucial role in the architecture of the rhetorical presentation.

We see here a process of transformation of forms, which Turner (1981, p. 155) explains when he writes that "one genre might supplant or replace another as the historically or situationally dominant form of 'social meta-commentary.' . . . New communicative techniques and media may make possible wholly unprecedented genres of cultural performance and thus new modes of self-understanding." Yet, in this newspaper presentation, a conscious analog of genres appears to be operating. José Limón (1986b, p. 27) comments on this type of process of transformation when he ana-lyzes Américo Paredes's *"With His Pistol in His Hand"* as a "transforming nar-rative response to the aesthetic influence of its scholarly subject, the bor-der ballad." He explains:

> In this fourth chapter Paredes offers, in his own restrained prose, an equivalent of the conversations that men may have after a *corrido* performance as they evaluate the *corrido*, its hero, its circumstances and try to get at the truth. As a post narrative review, Paredes' final chapter is like this kind of polyphonic conversation and as such an integral part of his total performance as it would be for a tradi-tional *corrido* sung to an audience. Hence, I would argue that even the seeming "review" character of Chapter IV recalls a *corrido* performance.

Similarly, the newspaper gives a rhetorical presentation that is analo-gous to the corrido performance situation. The text of the Norvell Report is juxtaposed to the *El Grito del Norte* editorial, a positioning that consti-tutes a statement/rebuttal type of contestation. Also, the biographies of the individuals give important background information, as listeners might conversationally discuss the actors in the story from their personal experi-ence. The poems, authored by family members or individuals from outside the immediate community, function as eulogies and statements of solidar-ity with the aggrieved parties. Within this presentation, which is designed to persuade the reader, the corrido by María Córdova is the focal point because it recalls an earlier time, one of oral performance, in which the ag-onistic dimensions of the Mexican/Chicano social drama resonate.

Earlier I noted that shared and consensual meaning was an important element of social drama. It is also an essential aspect of the teller/listener relationship, and its transformation into the rhetorical presentation in the newspaper must be looked at more closely. Renato Rosaldo's illuminating ethnographic work on Ilongot narrative (Rosaldo 1986) is instructive for this discussion because he details the difficulties that anthropologists, or outsiders, face when trying to listen to and understand the stories being told in an Ilongot storytelling session. From their etic perspective, he explains, outsiders are not privy to the emic view, that is, the internal knowledge of the wide range of history, social activity, and status demarcations that provide the necessary internal backdrop for understanding all narrative texts. Consequently, the outsider receives a thread of narration that appears to have multiple gaps and to make little sense. Because of the extreme isolation of the Ilongot culture, the visitors' lack of understanding becomes very apparent. Only to a limited extent can the outsider experience the shared and consensual meaning of the tribe.

Similarly, corridos and other genres of cultural performance are produced and performed within their own sphere of shared and consensual meaning. That María Córdova evokes the formulaic phrase *con su pistola en la mano* is a clear bid for the listener to recall the earlier corrido and to link the Canales/Córdova slayings to the conflict that gave, and continues to give, rise to forms of resistance in the Mexican/Chicano community. Those of us "in the know" will make the appropriate connections.

Yet this process of engaging consensual meaning also has a larger function. It serves to elicit communitas between the teller and the listener. Communitas is a concept that Turner describes as a key ingredient of human social activity; in fact, he remarks, "one might also postulate that the coherence of a completed social drama is itself a function of communitas" (Turner 1974, p. 50). Briefly, to recapitulate the argument in *The Ritual Process*, he explains, "the bonds of communitas are anti-structural in that they are undifferentiated, equalitarian, direct, nonrational (though not *irrational*), I-Thou or Essential We relationships, in Martin Buber's sense" (Turner 1969, pp. 46–47). In Turner's view, communitas is closely associated with liminality, that creative state of betwixt and between in which old paradigms transist into new ones.[4] Consequently, in the liminal state the claiming of a communal human identity is made possible; moreover, this process is basic to the sharing of consensus.

All of these ideas proceed out of Turner's differentiation between structure and antistructure. Structure involves all that constrains people's actions and defines their differences, while antistructure is a total and unmediated relationship between individuals, "a relationship which nevertheless does not submerge one in the other but safeguards their uniqueness in the very act of realizing their commonness" (Turner 1974, p. 298). He means by antistructure not a negative corollary to structure, but rather the positive, generative center of human activity. He concludes, then, that "man is both a structural and an anti-structural entity, who *grows* through antistructure and *conserves* through structure" (Turner 1974, p. 274).

That growth involves a creative projection, which is achieved through

the development of root metaphors, conceptual archetypes, and paradigms. For this discussion root metaphors are most important because
"root metaphors have a 'thusness' or 'thereness' from which many subsequent structures may be 'unpacked'" (Turner 1974, p. 50). The corrido is
transformed from a genre of cultural performance into a root metaphor
for the paradigmatic contestation between the Anglo American Other and
Mexicans on this side of the border. The root metaphor is part of a larger
model for activity that can be labeled a root paradigm. If we refer back to
Paredes's comments regarding the attitude that Mexicans assume when
"challenging a foreign people," his observation becomes an accurate assessment of a root paradigm that has informed much of Mexican/Chi-
cano cultural production. Turner (1974, p. 64) remarks that root paradigms "have reference not only to the current state of social relationships
existing or developing between actors, but also to the cultural goals,
means, ideas, outlooks, currents of thought, patterns of belief, and so on,
which enter into these relationships, interpret them, and incline them to
alliance or divisiveness."[5] The root paradigm that I have isolated here
clearly operates under these conditions and, it is important to keep in
mind, functions within the realm of communitas.

The change in function and presentation from the classic corrido form
to that of María Córdova's poem in *El Grito del Norte* raises important questions about the root metaphor and root paradigm of which the Mexi-
can/Chicano social drama is a part. The framing of the cultural performance seems to change as the notion of the political importance of an
event wanes. The deaths of Antonio and Rito never reach the mythic
significance of that of Gregorio Cortez. Nor are they considered by the
wider Chicano population to be role models worthy of emulation; they
have been, for all intents and purposes, lost to history. The political nature
of their deaths is secondary to the activity and response that they generated. The focus on the event appears to become subsumed by the rhetorical presentation itself. This movement away from hero and event as subject of the performance and as the model for action is evident in the
development of much of Chicano poetry emerging from this tradition.

For example, José Montoya's classic poem "El Louie" chronicles in ret-
rospective the life of Louie Rodríguez, "un vato de atolle." Without analyzing the complexities of this poem here, particularly since it has been
done so meticulously elsewhere by Juan Bruce-Novoa, Arturo Madrid,
Renato Rosaldo, and José Limón, it is necessary to note aspects important
to this discussion. First, the poem is not framed in a social drama context,
where redress is either desired or possible. Furthermore, Louie does not

perceive an Other as a foreign enemy threatening his integrity. I agree with Bruce-Novoa that the only Other that emerges for Louie is the seductive image of Humphrey Bogart, James Cagney, or George Raft, characters he has seen in the "mono" (movies), whom he emulates in his shifting postures of illusionary selfhood. Although "El Louie" maintains the element of narrativity (we are told of Louie's life from his high-riding days of "48 fleetline two-tone / buenas garras" [fine clothes] to his service in the Korean War and finally to his ignominious death in a rented room), no longer does a clear notion of social event or of affirming consensual values exist.

Yet "El Louie" does operate against a subtext of pachuco lore. The effect, however, is ironic and questionably affirmative. Even so, because of this subtext "El Louie" is still implicitly linked to a notion of community, if not communitas. Louie Rodríguez's life, moreover, bears out Paredes's view of the agonistic stance of the Mexican: "Being Mexican meant remaining inviolable in the face of overwhelming attack on one's personality" (Paredes 1979, p. 10). Despite his defeat, his drug addiction, and his marginality, Louie remains inviolable in the only way he knows how. But his defiant stance is different from that of Cortez or even of Canales and Córdova, who preceded him: Louie Rodríguez achieves selfhood only outside himself, from fantasy events, such as movies and their celluloid heroes. Louie deliberately moves outside the events of his own life to define himself. The irony of his life is that he turns to those consumer images of bravery fabricated by a society that impinges so destructively on his selfhood. By choosing these images, he could appear to entrench himself further in the domination that is making him extinct. Consequently, we could read Louie as indirectly accepting North American values, and his ignominious death in a rented room then would become an indirect "desertion under fire," to use Paredes's words. Yet Louie's shifting identities create a movable space for struggle and survival; his resistance is still communicated through narrative song to the "Baby Chukes."

The differences between the transformative development of the root metaphor and the root paradigm as seen in Cortez, Canales/Córdova, and Louie Rodríguez are suggestive. Whereas Gregorio Cortez, Antonio Córdova, and Rito Canales are shown within the events that define and link them to an implied communal center, Louie's link to this center is mediated and ultimately ironic.

Again Paredes helps us understand what has transpired in that transformation. In discussing the differences between folk poetry and what he terms sophisticated poetry, Paredes (1964, p. 225) comments that "in sophisticated poetry, . . . the tendency is toward more and more subtle and individual modes of expression once poetry has ceased to be performed and has become an act of private communication between poet and reader." "El Louie" is not performance in the folk poet's sense, nor is it a part of the type of social drama discussed above, although it is a poem that has been recorded and sung. (The musical rendering is lesser known and usually not taken into account.) Most importantly, "El Louie" moves toward those "subtle and individual modes of expression" in which Louie Rodríguez becomes an indeterminate symbol of resistance to an Other whose identity has become so blurred as to be rendered moot. Although a case can be made that the pachuco is an implicit resistance to Anglo American domination, the integration of Anglo American symbology into Louie's stance of selfhood complicates this interpretation. Louie Rodríguez's attitude of defiance is qualitatively different from Cortez's armed refusal of domination with a pistol or Córdova's with a pen. The defiance is turned inward against the self, not outward against an Other. Clearly, "El Louie" marks an important movement in the transformation of the root paradigm.[6]

In some ways, "El Louie" is a transitional poem: it displays some of the dramatistic elements of the corrido but does not show others, such as the creative, positive invocation of communitas. I have noted that communitas refers to the re-creation, always more or less provisionally, of a group that, for the time being, is strong and inviolable in the face of stress. The transformation I have been investigating appears to support the view that some poetic efforts develop out of, and support, communitas; that is, they are integrally linked to the root paradigm of the Mexican/Chicano social drama I have been discussing and of which the classic corrido is a core genre. Some, like "El Louie," bridge the gap between these and poetic efforts that veer away from this dramatistic paradigm. Take for example the poem "The Morning They Shot Tony Lopez, Barber and Pusher Who Went Too Far, 1958," by Gary Soto (1977, p. 11):

> When they entered through the back door,
> You were too slow in raising an arm
> Or thinking of your eyes refusing the light,
> Or your new boots moored under the bed,
> Or your wallet on the bureau, open
> And choking with bills,
> Or your pockets turned inside out, hanging breathless as
> tongues,

Or the vendor clearing his throat in the street,
Or your watch passed on to another's son,
Or the train to Los Banos,
The earth you would slip into like a shirt
And drift through forever.
When they entered, and shot once,
You twisted the face your mother gave
With the three, short grunts that let you slide
In the same blood you closed your eyes to.

Here the speaker almost clinically narrates the details of the scene: the wallet on the bureau, the boots moored under the bed, the blood. But Tony Lopez exists only as a "Pusher Who Went Too Far." He is not presented as a role model or as a catalyst for change. His community is absent except for the final action in which we see the traces of an absent mother and sense the racial blood, which he closed his eyes to. The poem's speaker does not articulate the event in its representative dimensions, but rather in its idiosyncratic force. The Spanish surname is the only link to a recognizable social milieu. Lopez's death becomes a general metaphor of violence in which community and any notion of redress are distanced and abstracted.

Similarly, in "History," a poem in the same volume, *The Elements of San Joaquín*, the speaker details his grandmother in all her particularity, "Loose skin / Of belly and breasts" (Soto 1977, pp. 40–41). But, most importantly, he articulates a severance from the events of her life and the community that she represented: "I do not know why / Her face shines / Or what goes beyond this shine, / Only the stories / That pulled her / From Taxco to San Joaquin, / Delano to Westside, / The places / In which we all begin." The events, or the "social drama or stories about them," to borrow Turner's phrase, are no longer immediate; they are representative only by their abstraction. "The places / in which we all begin" is a metaphorical declaration not based on immediate event or experience. Here there is no Other that causes a breach between the grandmother and the speaker, only time, which allows no redress. The shift from event poetry to, for lack of a better term, poetry of abstraction does not necessarily imply privilege of one form over the other. Rather, I contend that the movement out of event, out of the social drama mode and into a more abstract response to our communal reality, goes beyond a reframing of the Other and becomes a qualitative redefinition of self and of history.

The folklore, the corrido, and the stories have become abstracted and have changed in both functional and, perhaps, aesthetic value, although this discussion is not necessarily concerned with value. This is not a process limited to Mexicano/Chicanos; in fact this process of abstraction in art has been noted and commented on by many from José Ortega y Gasset to Irving Howe. Gerald Graff (1979, p. 2) offers a provocative observation of the situation in his *Literature against Itself*, in which he declares his "sympathy with the view that literature ought to play an adversary role in society. But recent social developments have opened up difficult questions about the adequacy of our ways of conceiving 'adversariness.'" To further illustrate his point, he draws on the ideas of Hans Magnus Enzensberger (1974, pp. 90–91; quoted in Graff 1979, p. 2):

> The capacity of the capitalist society to reabsorb, suck up, swallow, "cultural goods" of widely varying digestibility has enormously increased. Today the political harmlessness of all literary, indeed, all artistic products, is clearly evident: the very fact that they can be defined as such neutralized them. Their claim to be enlightening, their utopian surplus, their critical potential has shriveled to mere appearance . . . sooner or later, and usually sooner, by way of detours via advertising, design, and styling, the inventions become part and parcel of the consumer sphere.

These notions are suggestive of what we encounter in this discussion. What, then, is at stake when resistance-based forms become mere conventions? What shift in values occurs, and what implications does this shift hold for the future of the adversariness of Chicano literature? Certain questions also arise about the development of Chicano poetry out of the folk base. The first has to do with narrativity and the importance of consensual values in the creation of communitas. As poetry increasingly ceases to revolve around the politically laden event, will communitas survive? But the most important issue has to do with the disappearance of the Other and its effects on the distinction and raison d'être of Chicano poetry as it has developed through the various manifestations of the Mexicano/Chicano social drama.

If we consider the following poem, "With a Polka in His Hand," by Evangelina Vigil (1985, p. 25), the prospects are bright for the creative force of transformation. She aptly dedicates the poem to Don Américo Paredes:

tired out de todo el día
me senté a pistearme
una cuba libre
in a classy joint
with delicately leaved green plants
blossoming in all directions
and picturesque windows
brilliant mirrors
and a polished wooden antique bar

and I gazed out
through elongated window structures
framing like a picture
el patio en el mercado:
white, sun-bleached ladrillos cuadrados
whereupon
just one drink ago
troteaban los pies indios clad in dusty shoes
de aquel viejito
que se atravesaba en frente de la puerta
de la cantina cara y gringa—
yo
por un instante
esperando que él pasara
y él
contenido
en sus pensamientos claros
pushing with strong weathered brown arm
an ancient wooden cart
y en su mano izquierda
un radio de transistor
sí, un radio de transistor
aventando acordeón

and amazed
while just beginning to feel the buzz and warmth
I utter to myself out loud
"He's carrying a polka in his hand!"
and the anglo client seated next to me
glances over uncomprehendingly

and I think about Gregorio Cortez
and Américo Paredes
y en que la defensa cultural es permitida
and that calls for another drink
and another toast
y yo le digo a mí por el espejo
"¡ay, nomás!"
y me echo el trago[7]

Vigil draws a significant observation from Paredes's work on the corrido: "la defensa cultural es permitida" (the defense of culture is permitted) is a defiant stance against those who deny Chicano culture permission
to exist. Her scenario is a fitting analog to the larger social drama I have
been discussing. In this small drama, an old man is framed in the doorway
of "la cantina cara y gringa" (the costly Anglo American bar). In that liminal space, a polka bursts from the high-tech transistor radio he carries.
The polka, a derivative form of Texas/Mexican folk song, resonates back
to the early forms of the corrido and to those forms of cultural resistance
that survive as the contiguous agonistic relationship of the Mexican and
Anglo American Other continues to the present day; Cortez used a pistol,
Antonio Córdova used a pen, and the old man used a radio to express
their resistance. As the old man is framed, so, too, is the corrido reframed
in that oppositional image of him in the doorway of the Anglo American
bar. There is no audience to support and applaud her story, just a mirror
to which she lifts her glass and makes her toast. Consequently, only her
own image reflected in the mirror assents in return. Despite the solitary
image with which Vigil's poem ends, the transformation of the drama
from the classic border corrido to the María Córdova poem in *El Grito del
Norte* continues to be positive, creative, and generative.

This positive transformative attitude, it should be noted, occurs in
both poems through the female speaking voice. In the first, the maternal
role lends force to the persuasiveness of the use of the form; in the second,
the gendered stereotype is consternated as the speaker locates herself in a
"cantina," a space usually associated with males. In the following poem by
Lorna Dee Cervantes, the speaker questions the positioning of the woman
in the corrido form, and this becomes the site from which she levies her
transformation of the form. I have written about the gendered problematics of this poem elsewhere. In this context I want to underscore Cervantes's disaffection with the form in general. The following lines from
Cervantes's "Visions of Mexico While at a Writing Symposium in Port

Townsend, Washington" (1981, pp. 45–46) perhaps more aptly express the tension and agony that many contemporary poets face when trying to plumb the cultural space they have inherited:

> I don't want to pretend I know more
> and can speak all the names. I can't.
> My sense of this land can only ripple through my veins
> like the chant of an epic corrido.
> I come from a long line of eloquent illiterates
> whose history reveals what words don't say.
> Our anger is our way of speaking,
> the gesture is an utterance more pure than word.
> We are not animals
> but our senses are keen and our reflexes,
> accurate punctuation.
> All the knifings in a single night, low-voiced
> scufflings, sirens, gunnings . . .
> We hear them
> and the poet within us bays.

The attitude of resistance, which is a key ingredient of the social drama as it developed historically, is called on here to anchor the poet's inspiration. The dramatistic elements of the politically keyed situation are faint, and the Other is undefined, but the rage remains, and, therefore, the poetic impulse survives.

What happens when these elements are gone? Lentricchia (1983, p. 34) remarks that the ideological struggle at the level of discourse can lead to a "new organic ideology, where it might serve a different collective will." If this redefinition of the collective will is at the core of the transformation of symbols, metaphors, and genres of cultural performance, then we might deduce, as does Lentricchia, that "the fluidity, or undecidability, of the symbol is not, therefore, the sign of its social and political elusiveness but the ground of its historicity and of its flexible but also specific political significance and force." The answers to the questions posed by these considerations are not mine to give; they must be borne out by time. I can only reaffirm the force and importance of event in forging the uniqueness of Chicano literature as it has been underscored through history. As usual, this affirmation can best be given voice by a poet. In "Puente de cristal," Lucha Corpi (1980, pp. 78–80) writes of the influence that the life and death of her friend and mentor, the political activist Magdalena Mora, had on her work: "y yo por primera vez / dejé que mi palabra / apuntara hacia esenciales" (And for the first time / I allowed my word / to turn to essentials). For this poet, the choice is a conscious one—to let words point to the essential issues of communal existence or not. When and how, and if, this choice occurs forms the basis for understanding the evolution of Chicano poetry.

CHAPTER 3

"Mr.? . . ."

Rodriguez. The name on the door. The name on my passport. The name I carry from my parents—who are no longer my parents, in a cultural sense. This is how I pronounce it: Rich-heard Road-ree-guess. This is how I hear it most often.

The voice through a microphone says, "Ladies and Gentlemen, it is with pleasure that I introduce Mr. Richard Rodriguez."

RICHARD RODRIGUEZ
Hunger of Memory

"On Lies, Secrets, and Silence"

Hunger of Memory

AS AUTOBIOGRAPHY—

A COMPARATIVE PERSPECTIVE

Chicanos usually react vociferously to the mere mention of Richard Rodriguez. Some staunchly defend Rodriguez's right to "say what he says," and others condemn his ideas as reactionary. Both sides share an underlying assumption: all purport to know who Richard Rodriguez is. This assumption is not so surprising, given that we know him from his own words, his autobiography *Hunger of Memory*. I submit a counterthesis: we do not know who Richard Rodriguez is, precisely because of his first autobiography.[1]

When we speak about autobiographies, we tend to hold certain notions to be self-evident: (1) that we are given the sum total of a person's life and (2) that the account we are given is true. The first idea presupposes continuity, connectedness, coherence, and closure, while the second underscores the nature of the account as history, narration of events, and, therefore, truth. These commonly held aspects of autobiography are not necessarily so, however, because, as writing, autobiography is nothing other than story or narrative. Robert Scholes and Robert Kellogg (1966, p. 4) maintain that "for writing to be narrative no more and no less than a teller and a tale are required." The author selects incidents, events, and characters for narration and then formulates them into a structure of presentation—a fiction. But the complexity of the enterprise extends much deeper. The author gives us a mediated text, presenting him/herself to us through a constructed character who is, and at the same time is not, a projection of the person. So we now have three personae to deal with: (1) the actual person writing the story, (2) the character devised in the story to carry on the work (observation, narration, commentary) of the writer, and (3) the image of the writer, which is a combination of points 1 and 2 and is created in the storytelling relation of writer, narrator, and text.

Michel Foucault has coined the term "author-function" to refer to this complicated phenomenon, which pertains to all narrative texts. He cautions that "the proper name and the name of an author oscillate between the poles of description and designation, and granting that they are linked to what they name, they are not totally determined either by their descriptive or designative functions" (Foucault 1977, p. 121).

These considerations lead us to ask certain questions about the reactions with which this discussion opened: the Richard Rodriguez whom we assume to know may not be the Richard Rodriguez who wrote the book and may not be the Rich-heard Road-ree-guess who narrates the story. Rather, we are presented with a complex author-function in which we become implicated as readers and which takes into account the author as cultural actuator-producer in society, motivator and writer of the story, and fictional character as well. Rodriguez, like all autobiographers, is a writer of various texts among which his autobiography is just one.

Let me recount a portion of Foucault's argument regarding the four features that comprise the author-function (Foucault 1977, pp. 124–130). First, for Foucault texts have become "objects of appropriation"; once texts became legal entities they became forms of property. The text took on this status when the author became the agent legally liable for its creation. Up until that time, he argues, the status of a text was governed by the following social designations: sacred/profane, lawful/unlawful, and religious/blasphemous. But the act of writing now exists as an order of property. Given the risk of transgressing rules of ownership and copyright laws, writing has been transformed from a social force born in political and religious forms to an entity of property—an objectified personal possession protected by law.

Second, the author-function, Foucault explains, is not the same for all discourses. Take, for example, folktales or epics. In these, the anonymity of the author is a given fact. We do not know who originated *Beowulf* or *The Song of Roland*, yet these texts exist with an author-function in which the author is not designated. Nevertheless, for the most part, literary works achieve a measure of their authenticity from the reputation of the author. This ancient practice of identifying the text with the author means that a text is usually dominated by the authority of the author. Consider the force that Dr. Benjamin Spock's various books on childrearing exerted in the fifties. Even in modern literary criticism, one of the first tasks of the scholarly endeavor is to authenticate the author of a text. A complicated interrelationship exists between the force or value of a text and the author.

Third, the author-function is related to the standing of the author within both the literary community and society in general. There is an entity whom we call author. The description of this persona comes from judgments as to his/her individual creativity, intelligence, and seriousness.

What must be underscored here is that this rational entity is a by-product or projection, "in terms always more or less psychological, of our way of handling texts: in the comparisons we make, the traits we extract as pertinent, the continuities we assign, or the exclusions we practice" (Foucault 1977, p. 127). Thus the entity "Ernest Hemingway" became the stylist of his generation and his texts the models for a number of aspiring writers.

Just as the texts themselves account for the constructed author, this author gives form and direction to his/her texts. The author validates the presence or absence of events within a text, their presentation, distortion, or identification. In this context, scholarly referral to a writer's biography or written records gives us clues about the author's position within society: class status, point of view, or social preferences. In this way, contradictions present in the texts can be reconciled through the definition of personal, historical material.

Finally, texts contain numerous grammatical signs, such as pronouns or verb forms, and nongrammatical signs which refer to the author. In many instances this referral is not a simple one, for these signs, Foucault (1977, p. 129) explains, stand for "a second-self whose similarity to the author is never fixed and undergoes considerable alteration within the course of a single book. It would be as false to seek the author in relation to the actual writer as to the fictional narrator." By noting this multiplicity of selves, Foucault (1977, p. 130) underscores the fact that "all discourse that supports this 'author-function' is characterized by this plurality of egos."

We answer the question of who Richard Rodriguez is by asserting that he is all of the above. Most readers and critics of Rodriguez's book have confined their analyses and commentaries to only the first and third of these author-functions: his role in marketing his personal property, *Hunger of Memory*, and the social and political standing that he has accrued through this marketing activity, as well as the way in which his text has been handled by others. (It has been touted as the definitive statement concerning bilingual education and affirmative action.) Foucault's argument suggests that we have been dealing with a somewhat truncated Richard Rodriguez, whose complexities of author-function have not been sufficiently addressed. The following comments are intended to fill this gap.

Let us turn to the question of the authenticity of the text in regard to the authority of the author and how that authority relates to the second-self that emerges in the presentation of a text. For our purposes, let us call this latter persona the narrator (although obviously the narrator is implied in some texts). Seymour Chatman in *Story and Discourse* (1978) uses Aristotle to illustrate his argument on the need to delineate the authority of the author. In *The Rhetoric,* Aristotle avers that "it is not true, as some writers on the art maintain, that the probity of the speaker contributes nothing to his persuasiveness; on the contrary, we might almost affirm that his character (ethos) is the most potent of all the means to persuasion" (Cooper 1960, pp. 8–9). Chatman (1978, p. 227) draws the following corollary from Aristotle's remarks: "Insofar as a narrative is true, that is, history, the narrator seeks by usual rhetorical means to establish the reliability of his ethos."

In autobiography, however, we have the intersection of two types of narrative: history and fiction. Whereas Chatman distinguishes between historical truth and fictional truth, I concur with others, such as Hayden White, who believe that all narrative, whether fictional or historical, is governed by a "semblance of veracity" because narrative, to be brief, is interpretation.[2] In autobiography, then, where the criterion of truth is so basic to its definition as genre, we are actually dealing with a semblance of truth, since the text is but one perspective on a series of events. Aristotle's admonition that the probity of character is essential to the authority and force of persuasion regarding truth becomes even more complex when we consider Foucault's argument that the speaker is really various strata of author-functions, of which the narrator is just one.

But we must deal with the narrator and his probity and qualifications of authority within his text. I submit that the narrator, Rich-heard Road-ree-guess, is an unreliable narrator whose position of probity can only be assessed in ironic stance to his text. Moreover, I argue that the narrative contains a sustained discourse of contradiction between point of view and the narrator's own words and observations, which nullifies the consistency of the narrator's perceptions and, thus, belies the professed truth of his narrative. Seymour Chatman (1978, p. 234) asks, "What precisely is the domain of unreliability? It is the discourse, that is, the view of what happens or what the existents are like, not the personality of the narrator." Consequently, the judgment that Richard Rodriguez is an unreliable narrator is not a personal condemnation, but rather a comment on the internal configuration of the narrative. I will now assess more accurately the semblance of veracity that this text proposes, first by analyzing the narrator's reliability and second by comparing this with other autobiographical texts.

ON LIES AND SECRETS

The dedication in *Hunger of Memory* is a dialogue in which the mother boasts about her son's Ph.D. to her friends, while in private asking her son whether someone has done something to him at Berkeley. In the dialogue, in which both father and mother participate, Richard only utters one abrupt word, "No" (Rodriguez 1983).[3] This excerpt is clearly intended to show his parents' failure to understand their son's ambiguous position in society, yet Rodriguez ends with the sobering tribute: "For her and for him—to honor them." I suggest that the dedication calls forth several major contradictions that are not resolved in the text. The first is the critical stance the dedicator takes toward his untutored parents' lack of understanding, a point of view that is juxtaposed to the written honor given them in the dedication. Second, the mother's reference to a hurt at Berkeley formulates an expectation of information that is never given overt voice in the text, although it is clear that Rodriguez was wounded psychically and perhaps sexually by his education. And third, despite his purported facility with language, which Rodriguez exalts in his narrative, his parents are the expressive ones here; in the face of their command, he can only answer, "No."

Rodriguez attempts to return to his origins in order to situate his tale. This return is significant because it implies an impulse to explain what has remained unexplained; that is, to provide in a reconstituted text something that has been missing. The life as lived and the life as remembered amount to two different texts, which must be reconciled, as they must in all auto-biography. For the reader to whom the text is directed, the pattern of omission becomes an invaluable map to delineating the ethos of that narrative.[4]

Foucault (1977, p. 135) explains the phenomenon of omission and the need to return and add the missing information as "always a return to a text in itself, specifically, to a primary and unadorned text with particular attention to those things registered in the interstices of the text, its gaps and absences." Just as the narrator must return to the text of his life, we must return to the text that he formulates in order to perceive his life accurately. Repetitive omissions are just as important as repeated facts. Especially when the narrator is unreliable, foregrounding the covert is necessary to understanding the overt. Because doing so allows us to achieve a critical stance toward the narrator, let us return to our preliminary analysis of the dedication.

We garner from the covert discourse an element of contradiction that must be unraveled for us to situate the narrator in relation to his text. Consequently, we approach the first chapter with a much deeper understanding of the self-conscious, ironic pose that the narrator assumes—the point of view belies the written text.

Rodriguez begins the prologue with a reference to Caliban. He takes

Caliban's desire to steal Prospero's books as the beginning of his tale of education (1983, p. 3): "I have taken Caliban's advice. I have stolen their books. I will have some run of this isle . . . (In Beverly Hills will this monster make a man.)" Both Ramón Saldívar (1990) and José David Saldívar have written elucidating commentaries on the Shakespearean reference in this autobiography. I need not recapitulate their arguments here. I would like to pursue a corollary argument in which Rodriguez's self-association with the resistance of Caliban is uncovered to reveal an association with Prospero, the colonial usurper, instead. Let us consider Rodriguez's parents, whose silent resistance to their son more closely resembles Caliban's inarticulate anger at his dispossession of his island by Prospero. Caliban never does steal Prospero's books, but those contested volumes are not the only "book" to have been stolen. Prospero has usurped Caliban's mother Sycorax's powers and from that discourse of magic has structured his alternate kingdom on the island.

Caliban's inheritance, his "book," has been stolen, and it is Prospero who has taken the power for his own gain. Despite the reference, it appears that Rodriguez is not the Caliban of the tale, but rather the Prospero whose magic is founded on the loss of another. It can be argued that Rodriguez has taken the magic away from others, from his parents. Even Rodriguez realizes that his parents are the originators of his self, but he has dispossessed them of this role (1983, p. 4): "Rodriguez, the name on the door. The name on my passport. The name I carry from my parents—who are no longer my parents in the cultural sense." Like Prospero, who must constantly return to the originators of his magic in order to plumb its depths, Rodriguez cannot separate himself from his origins, no matter how primitive they may seem. (Consider the fact that the subject of most of his writing, both autobiographical and journalistic, is Mexico and Mexicanness.) After all, Prospero succeeds only in establishing a "rough magic," and his usurpation of powers ultimately isolates him from civilization. The problem for Prospero resides in his inability to be totally magical or totally civilized. He comes to understand that he must relinquish Caliban's birthright in order to effect the marriage of his daughter Miranda and his return to Milan to claim his proper kingdom.

If Caliban has been retrieved as the quintessential Third World subject (Fernández Retamar 1989) by theorists of the Americas, Rodriguez's displeasure over his cultural identification with Mexican language and culture does not align him with the figure of Caliban at all. In fact, it appears that Rodriguez is profoundly confused about which "book" he desires and which kingdom he seeks.

The only return for Rodriguez would be back into the familial womb, a move he overtly shuns. He views his parents as inarticulate Calibans to his Prospero and does not understand that his "rough magic" cannot find natural expression until original rights have been realigned. Instead, he lauds the dispossession of his parents and exalts his rough magic over their sacrifice: he cannot hear the eloquence of their resistant silence. Overtly, the narrative constitutes a polemical argument about the need to dispossess certain cultural intimacies in order to achieve public identity. Although Rodriguez has superficially used the Caliban story to ground his narrative, a much deeper signification exists. Even in the first lines of the text, a subtext is working in which the overt presentation of self is belied by the covert logical implications of his own words.

Parents are central to the subtext of contradiction that infuses *Hunger of Memory*. Just two examples are sufficient to argue the case. In the chapter "Aria," the narrator tells us of his move from Spanish to English and, ultimately, to alienation from his family. He characterizes his parents as the embodiment of that pull into the family womb: "You belong here. We are family members. Related. Special to one another. Listen!" (p. 18). But Richard does not listen: he chooses to be outside, not inside; to speak English, not Spanish. The basic contradiction lies not in the language, but rather in the opposing characterizations of his parents and in the perception he chooses to accept.

We are told how his parents reacted to the discrimination of the 1950s by assuming a stance of dignity and power. They were viewed as different and made their differentness a point of pride, not subjugation: "My mother and father were more annoyed than intimidated by those two or three neighbors who tried initially to make us unwelcome" (p. 12). They reacted with strength: "They regarded the people at work, the faces in the crowds, as very distant from us. They were the others, *los gringos*. That term was interchangeable in their speech with another, even more telling, *los americanos*" (p. 12). Richard also remembers another reaction, which we perceive through his point of view: "In public, my father and mother spoke a hesitant, accented, not always grammatical English. And they would have to strain—their bodies tense—to catch the sense of what was rapidly said by *los gringos*" (p. 13).

Despite the next sentences, which counterpoint their hesitancy in English with the easy flow of their Spanish, the overriding impression one extracts from the episode is the narrator's embarrassment about the spectacle he feels his parents are making. Thus, the consistent pull of his parents toward a pride and recognition of their familial and linguistic legacy only drives the narrator further away. Theirs, the narrator intimates, is a "senti-mental" protectiveness, which he must escape. Consequently, in the next part we are told, "Fortunately, my teachers were unsentimental about their responsibility" (p. 19). The covert juxtaposition is clear: his parents are sentimental and have failed in their responsibility to him. Words of praise come only for his English-speaking teachers, who facilitated his accep-tance into the ranks of those Anglos who viewed his parents as humiliat-ing themselves. Richard has made himself one of these. The dedication "For her and for him—to honor them" now fully contradicts the sem-blance of veracity presented in the text.

Moving to the final chapter, we see the culmination of the stance that the narrator has assumed in opposition to his parents. At the annual Christmas dinner, Richard sits in isolation. Mother and siblings are pre-sented to us as if through a telescopic camera lens—the cameraman is far away, but the magnification brings us closer. Rodriguez is the objective an-thropologist who itemizes his observations of his informants. The dis-tance between himself and his family concurs with that introduced in the first chapter. They speak to him, but he maintains his distance and differ-ence from them. He denies them access to himself: "'Are you writing a book?' . . . I say 'Yes.' 'Well, well, well. Let's see it. Is it going to be a love story? A romance? What is it about?'" (1983, p. 192). Richard does not an-swer. He assumes they will not understand and consequently sees his father as confused, unable to hear, unable to speak since "his English is bad." Again, Richard regards his parents from the position of self-imposed isolation. His judgmental stance, implied in Chapter 1, becomes overt in the last chapter: "And his eyes move from face to face. Sometimes I feel that he is looking at me, I look over to see him, and his eyes dart away the second after I glance" (p. 193).

Richard has become the intimidating Anglo who discomfits his father in human interactions. Once again, the subtext of contradiction imposes itself in the final paragraph. Richard's mother tells him to take a jacket out to his father. He places it over his father's shoulders. "I feel the thinness of his arms. He turns. He asks if I am going home now too. It is, I realize, the only thing he has said to me all evening" (p. 195). The father's impassive strength has needed no words to be consciously felt by the rest of the family, yet for Richard the silence constitutes a personal act of exclusion. Under closer analysis, however, it is not the father who has failed to com-municate, but Richard who has not addressed his own father directly. The omission of his own role in the incident is very significant. As in Chapter 1, the subtext supports the idea that his parents were somehow to blame for his social and educational difficulties; in this last scenario, the narrator adds to that perspective. His parents and family, it is intimated, bear the onus of his alienation and so are condemned by the impersonal camera eye that he has become.

Underneath the pitying, self-professed love for his parents, a virulent anger emerges in the subtext. Richard perceives his father's disapproval through the old man's silence, but Richard and his father become parallel figures in the last chapter. Richard uses withdrawal and silence to condemn his parents for some vague transgression: "'What is new with you?' My mother looks up from her ironing to ask me. (In recent years she has taken to calling me Mr. Secrets, because I tell her so little about my work in San Francisco—this book she must suspect I am writing.) 'Nothing much,' I respond" (p. 186). Richard deliberately withholds information; moreover, the information he withholds is not limited to his work. The mother's question resonates from the initial question heard in the dedication: "Did somebody hurt you at Berkeley?" The implication is clear. He withholds from his mother and from us, the reader, vital information about who he is, what he does, and what has happened to him.

It is significant, therefore, that the chapter "Mr. Secrets" is overtly concerned with his work but covertly alludes to a personal crisis that, in part, takes place at Berkeley. We are never specifically to know the secret but, covertly, the issue is clear. The words used to describe his "secret" activity or writing are highly charged. He laments: "They never are tempted to believe that public life can also be intimate" and "With my mother and father I scorn those who attempt to create an experience of intimacy in public. . . . There are things so deeply personal that they can be revealed only to strangers. I believe this, I continue to write" (1983, pp. 184–185). The succeeding reference to psychiatry with its emphasis on the mind and the uncovering of associations provides a lead-in for the associations that his words invite. The juxtaposition between public and private, between intimacy and knowledge, leads to one conclusion—a private intimacy has yet to become public, and, in the mystification of events that is seen in the composition of Rodriguez's text, the secret has yet to be overtly named.[5]

All genres require certain properties in order to assure clarity and produce an effect. In autobiography, whose genre definition, as already noted, is inextricably linked to character (ethos), coherence and consistency are necessary properties. In some cases these properties are sufficiently altered as to cause the reader concern. Frank Kermode (1980, p. 81) characterizes this situation as one in which a conflict exists "between narrative sequence (or whatever it is that creates the 'illusion of narrative sequence') and what

I shall loosely, but with pregnant intention, call secrets." He refers to two conflicting discourses in a narrative, one that proceeds sequentially toward clarity and an Other that leans toward "secrecy, toward distortions which cover secrets." In fact, in some texts, the conflict between the two discourses is so great as to discomfit. "Secrets are at odds with sequence," Kermode (1980, p. 82) tells us. And in characterization sequence refers to consistency.

Therefore, in autobiography, where the probity of one character determines the persuasiveness of a text, the issues of opposing discourses are acutely important and problematic. The attentive reader is compelled to read not only the manifest portions of a text, but its less-manifest portions as well, its secrets. The reading seems to run counter to the natural sense of the text. This situation is underscored in autobiography, where as readers we are called upon to believe the sequence of events or character because the narrator, who was there, tells us that it is so. The consistency of characterization is a basic property of autobiography and essential for the sake of clarity and effect.

In *Hunger of Memory* we are dealing with an unreliable narrator. Kermode (1980, p. 86) comments on the problem that such narrators present: "The more unreliable they are, the more they can say that seems irrelevant to, or destructive of, the proprieties. They break down the conventional relationship between sequential narrative and history-likeness, with its arbitrary imposition of truth; they complicate the message." The narrator, Richard Rodriguez, presents us with an "illusion of narrative sequence," but he complicates his own message. We cannot read *Hunger of Memory* without taking into account the continuous subtext of contradiction or secrets because these secrets form compelling associations of their own: they are "secret invitations to interpretation rather than appeals to consensus" (Kermode 1980, p. 89). Rodriguez's emphasis on secrets actually leads us into a deeper subtext of counterdiscourse in which his authority as author is questioned.

Thus, going back to the query that began this discussion—"Who is Richard Rodriguez?"—we can only answer that we do not know. More importantly, the text tells us that Richard Rodriguez doesn't know either. Consequently, when the narrator says, "If my story is true, I trust it will resonate with significance for other lives," we are profoundly confused. Close reading has called into question the truth of the text and the identity of the narrator himself. Consternation, not truth, resonates in this text. As autobiography, *Hunger of Memory* appears to have confounded the genre itself.

ON SILENCE

Frederic Jameson in his *Marxism and Form* (1971) cautions that the critical enterprise must always take into account the literary tradition from which the text emerges. In a similar vein, Foucault (1977, p. 131) points to the "initiators of discursive practices" who constitute the background of literary tradition. One cannot fully comprehend the effect of *Hunger of Memory* as autobiography without considering it in relation to these other initiators of discursive practices. As an ethnic American autobiographer, Rodriguez is not alone. In fact, a wide field of writing is similar at least in content and deals with the reconciliation of the self within a multicultural framework. For this discussion, I have chosen three contemporary autobiographical texts as points of comparative analysis: Maya Angelou's *I Know Why the Caged Bird Sings* (1971), N. Scott Momaday's *The Names* (1976), and Maxine Hong Kingston's *The Woman Warrior: Memoirs of a Girlhood among Ghosts* (1977).[6]

I suggest that these three texts and Rodriguez's fall into two categories of writing—that which presents visual analogs to the experience of interiority (or the self) and that which functions as oral analogs. Walter J. Ong argues convincingly that the author, born and bred into a written or chirographic language tradition, can never understand the organic, totalizing sense that the oral wor·! had for preliterate people. In fact, he believes the knowledge of this loss constitutes the price one pays for literacy. Yet he also suggests that through literacy one can approximate the oral past: "Literacy can be used to reconstruct for ourselves the pristine human consciousness which was not literate at all—at least to reconstruct this consciousness pretty well, though not perfectly (we can never forget enough of our familiar present to reconstitute in our minds any past in its full integrity)" (Ong 1982, p. 15). Visual and oral analogs are modes used to restructure and approach this past.

Ong (1982, pp. 72–73) states that visual and oral cognitive processes differ significantly: "Sight isolates, sound incorporates. Whereas sight situates the observer outside what he views, at a distance, sound pours into the hearer." Thus vision dissects, while sound unites. "When I hear," Ong tells us, "I gather sound simultaneously from every direction at once: I am at the center of my auditory world, which envelops me, establishing me at a kind of core of sensation and existence. . . . You can immerse yourself in hearing, in sound. There is no way to immerse yourself similarly in sight." Thus the visual experience can be understood as a duality: internal and external. The self is internal, and all else exists in external relation to the self.

Conversely, the process of sound places the communal person at the nexus of the entire cosmos; as Ong explains, "the field of sound is not spread out before me, but is all around me."

Richard Rodriguez and Maya Angelou present visual analogs to the experience of interiority and exteriority, yet these analogs differ in effect. Rodriguez distances himself from the events and emotions he relates, thus maintaining himself as the individual center of his narrative. Angelou incorporates into her visual analog a technique that minimizes distance and produces a measure of collectivity. Angelou's presentation is oriented toward performance, and the performance aspect is acutely significant because she uses it to draw the reader into the event she is narrating, thus producing a sense of interaction between narrator and reader. The result is an illusion of communal experience garnered within the visual analog technique.

Note the difference between these two excerpts. The first is Rodriguez's account of the conflict he feels toward his religious life:

> When I go to church on Sunday I am forced to recognize a great deal about myself. I would rather go to a high ceremonial mass, reap for an hour or two its communal assurance. The sentimental solution would be ideal: to remain a liberal Catholic and to worship at a traditional mass. But now that I no longer live as a Catholic in a Catholic world, I cannot expect the liturgy—which reflects and cultivates my faith—to remain what it was. I will continue to go to the English mass. I will go because it is my liturgy. I will, however, often recall with nostalgia the faith I have lost. And I will be uneasy knowing that the old faith was lost as much by *choice* as it was inevitably lost.
> (p. 107)

The following is the culminating scene of an incident at church that Angelou recalls from her childhood. Bailey, her brother, has moved Angelou to the point of suppressed hysteria and laughter with his comments about Sister Monroe's wild devotion:

> While the sounds in the Church were increasing, Elder Thomas made the regrettable mistake of increasing his volume too. Then suddenly, like a summer rain, Sister Monroe broke through the cloud of people trying to hem her in, and flooded up to the pulpit. She didn't stop this

time, but continued immediately to the altar, bound for Elder Thomas, crying, "I say, preach it!"

Bailey said out loud, "Hot dog" and "Damn" and "She's going to beat his butt."

But Reverend Thomas didn't intend to wait for that eventuality, so as Sister Monroe approached the pulpit from the right he started descending from the left. He was not intimidated by his change of venue. He continued preaching and moving. He finally stopped right in front of the collection table, which put him almost in our laps, and Sister Monroe rounded the altar on his heels, followed by the deacons, ushers, some unofficial members and a few of the bigger children.

Just as the Elder opened his mouth, pink tongue waving, and said, "Great God of Mount Nebo," Sister Monroe hit him on the back of his head with her purse. Twice. Before he could bring his lips together, his teeth fell, no, actually his teeth jumped, out of his mouth.

The grinning uppers and lowers lay by my right shoe, looking empty and at the same time appearing to contain all the emptiness in the world. . . . (pp. 35–36)

In the excerpt from *Hunger of Memory*, the narrator has dissected and analyzed his religious experience. He is telling us his conclusions about his religious past and present. Rodriguez's text is basically polemical: it lays out an argument and draws conclusions. Angelou, however, demonstrates what that religious past has been. Aside from the distinct paucity of humor in Rodriguez's narrative and Angelou's highly effective use of humor, the principal factor differentiating these texts is the narrators' stance in regard to their experience. Angelou's narrator projects herself into the consciousness of an eight-year-old child. We are told the event through the child's point of view, which draws the reader into the immediacy of the action, and yet we are pulled back smoothly and appropriately to the adult perspective. In other words, Angelou's narrator is involved in the event. In contrast, Rodriguez's narrator stands aloof from his experience. He is the sole interpreter of the event, while Angelou allows the reader to participate and thus to add his or her own interpretation to that of the narrator. An illusion of shared community and opinion results from the performance-oriented text.

Another aspect of the performance-oriented text differentiates the visual analog techniques employed by Angelou and Rodriguez. Angelou projects the narrator's point of view into that of an eight-year-old child, a twelve-year-old adolescent, and a fifteen-year-old young woman. In this way, she can relate highly personal and sensitive experiences, which would have been difficult to tell from an adult's point of view. Thus we are privy to her rape as an eight-year-old, her life as a runaway living in a junkyard, and her anxieties about her sexual identity, which result in her premature motherhood. The narrator's reliability is assured because she draws the reader into the consciousness of the individual at the time of the event. There is no provision for secrets within this type of narrative. Rodriguez, however, uses narrative distancing to withhold rather than to reveal information. The provision for secrets is a by-product of the polemical, argumentative stance.

Yet the narratives that Angelou and Rodriguez construct are similar in one important aspect—the presentation of time. Visual analogs are tied to conventional notions of time: the artificial ways in which we have learned to demarcate time through calendar days, months, or years. Both Angelou and Rodriguez use this conventional time frame to present their lives. Rodriguez gives us chapter designations such as "Aria" or "Credo" within which he reports his experiences chronologically. Angelou narrates her life from childhood until adolescence in *I Know Why the Caged Bird Sings*, only to take up where she left off in her next volume. Thus she constructs a chronological autobiographical series.

The presentation of time differentiates visual from oral analogs. Ong (1982, p. 76) explains that "sound is an event in time, and 'time marches on,' relentlessly, with no stop or division. Time is seemingly tamed if we treat it spatially on a calendar or the face of a clock, where we can make it appear as divided into separate units next to each other. But this also falsifies time. Real time has no divisions at all, but is uninterruptedly continuous." Momaday and Kingston treat time as a continuous flow in which space is a factor of time, not vice versa, as in the visual analog. For this reason, Momaday can project himself back in time to the arbor that carries within it the sounds of his ancestors, the breath of his racial and communal life. In his narrative, space equals sound: "There seems a stillness at noon, but this is illusion: the landscape rises and falls, ringing" (p. 4). And Momaday continues:

> These are the things I know: the slow, summer motion of
> the air, the shadows that gather upon the walls, birds criss-
> crossing at the screen, the rhythms within me. And I know
> the voices of my parents, of my grandmother, of others.

Their voices, their words, English and Kiowa—and the
silences that lie about them—are already the element of
my mind's life.

   Zei-dl-bei. Brush the flies away.

   Had I known it, even then language bore all the names
of my being. (pp. 7–8)

Rodriguez cannot intimate the resonances of being that Momaday so
clearly captures. Spanish is not a part of his being anymore, and for this
reason, he tells us, he feels the loss of his "intimate" private life and feels
alienated from his parents. Let us compare these two accounts of their
grandmothers. Rodriguez recounts:

   The last time I saw my grandmother I was nine years old.
   I can tell you some of the things she said to me as I stood
   by her bed. I cannot, however, quote the message of intimacy she conveyed with her voice. She laughed, holding
   my hand. Her voice illumined disjointed memories as it
   passed them again. She remembered her husband, his
   green eyes, the magic name of Narciso. His early death.
   She remembered the farm in Mexico. The eucalyptus
   nearby. (Its scent, she remembered, like incense.) She remembered the family cow, the bell round its neck heard
   miles away. A dog. She remembered working as a seam-
   stress. How she'd leave her daughters and son for long
   hours to go into Guadalajara to work. And how my
   mother would come running toward her in the sun—her
   bright yellow dress—to see her return. *Mmmaaammmááááá,*
   the old lady mimicked her daughter (my mother) to her
   son. She laughed. There was the snap of a cough. An aunt
   came into the room and told me it was time I should
   leave. "You can see her tomorrow," she promised. And so
   I kissed my grandmother's cracked face. And the last thing
   I saw was her thin, oddly youthful thigh, as my aunt re-
   arranged the sheet on the bed.

   At the funeral parlor a few days after, I knelt with my
   relatives during the rosary. . . . When I went up to look at
   my grandmother, I saw her through the haze of a veil
   draped over the open lid of the casket. Her face appeared
   calm—but distant and unyielding to love. It was not the
   face I remembered seeing most often. It was the face she
   made in public when the clerk at Safeway asked her some

question and I would have to respond. It was her public
face the mortician had designed with his dubious art.
(pp. 39–40)

And Momaday remembers:

It seems reasonable to suppose that I visited my great-
grandmother on other occasions, but I remember only this
once, and I remember it very well. My father leads me into
her room. It is dark and close inside, and I cannot see until my eyes become accustomed to the dim light. There is
a certain odor in the room and not elsewhere in the house,
the odor of my great-grandmother's old age. It is not un-
pleasant, but it is most particular and exclusive, as much
hers as is her voice or her hair or the nails of her hands.
Such a thing has not only the character of great age but
something also of the deep self, of one's own dignity and
well-being. Because of this, I believe, this old blind woman
is like no one I have ever seen or shall ever see. To a child
her presence is formidable. My father is talking to her in
Kiowa, and I do not understand what is being said, only
that the talk is of me. She is seated on the side of the bed,
and my father brings me to stand directly in front of her.
She reaches out for me and I place my hands in hers. *Eh
neh neh neh neh.* She begins to weep very softly in a high,
thin, hollow voice. Her hands are little and soft, so soft
that they seem not to consist in flesh and bone, but in the
softest fiber, cotton or fine wool. Her voice is so delicate,
so surely expressive of her deep feelings. Long afterwards I
think: That was a wonderful and beautiful thing that happened in my life. There, on that warm, distant afternoon:
an old woman and a child, holding hands across the generations. There is great good in such a remembrance. I cannot imagine that it might have been lost upon me. (p. 65)

Rodriguez views language as speech, while Momaday and Kingston
perceive language as sound. The first perspective is linked to grammatical
and lexical boundaries; the second obliterates such designations. For Momaday and Kingston, the old English term "winged-words" closely describes their conception. Words are sense-sounds, incorporating all the
five senses into the communication. Consequently, Kingston can sense the
significance of her mother's Chinese medical degree:

Once in a long while, four times so far for me, my mother
brings out the metal tube that holds her medical diploma.
On the tube are gold circles crossed with seven red lines
each—"joy" ideographs in abstract. There are also little
flowers that look like gears for a gold machine. According
to the scraps of labels with Chinese and American addresses, stamps, and post-marks, the family airmailed the
can from Hong Kong in 1950. It got crushed in the middle,
and whoever tried to peel the labels off stopped because
the red and gold paint came off too, leaving silver scratches
that rust. Somebody tried to pry the end off before discovering that the tube pulls apart. When I open it, the
smell of China flies out, a thousand-year-old bat flying
heavy-headed out of the Chinese caverns where bats are as
white as dust, a smell that comes from long ago, far back
in the brain. (p. 67)

Momaday and Kingston use sense-sound in order to imaginatively project themselves, their sense of self. Momaday declares:

I invented history. In April's thin white light, in the white
landscape of the Staked Plains, I looked for tracks among
the tufts of coarse, brittle grass, amid the stones, beside
the tangle of dusty hedges. When I look back upon those
days—days of infinite promise and steady adventure and
the certain sanctity of childhood—I see how much was
there in the balance. The past and the future were simply
the large contingencies of a given moment; they bore upon
the present and gave it shape. One does not pass through
time, but time enters upon him, in his place. As a child, I
knew this surely, as a matter of fact; I am not wise to
doubt it now. Notions of the past and future are essen-
tially notions of the present. In the same way an idea of
one's ancestry and posterity is really an idea of the self.
About this time I was formulating an idea of the self.
(p. 97)

In speaking of his mother, he raises the same point: "She imagined who
she was. This act of the imagination was, I believe, among the most important events of my mother's early life, as later the same essential act was
to be among the most important of my own" (p. 25).

The imagining of oneself constitutes power. Kingston describes the difficulty in reconciling her two selves, the Chinese and the American:

> I could not understand "I." The Chinese "I" has seven strokes, intricacies. How could the American "I," assuredly wearing a hat like the Chinese, have only three strokes, the middle so straight? Was it out of politeness that this writer left off strokes the way a Chinese has to write her own name small and crooked? No, it was not politeness; "I" is a capital and "you" is lower-case. I stared at that middle line and waited so long for its black center to resolve into tight strokes and dots that I forgot to pronounce it. The other troublesome word was "here," no strong consonant to hang on to, and so flat, when "here" is two mountainous ideographs. (pp. 193–194)

Kingston uses her imagination to project a sense of self, which she sees as emerging, like the smell of China from her mother's medical degree, from the talk-story of her parents and from the talk-story of her own autobiography. As she says, talk-story has the power to remind. And Kingston reminds herself of all her predecessors, imagining that they make up the multistroked self she creates in her narrative. Thus Kingston is Fa Mu Lan, the warrior woman of Chinese mythology on whose back were carved the accusations of oppression of her people; she is the strong-willed Brave Orchid, her mother, who labored as a doctor in China and as a laundress in the United States. But then she is also Moon Orchid, her aunt, whose displacement from China brings on her madness. Kingston is all of these selves. She is their spokeswoman and powerful agent: "The swordswoman and I are not so dissimilar. May my people understand the resemblance soon so that I can return to them. What we have in common are the words at our backs. The idioms for *revenge* are 'report a crime' and 'report to five families.' The reporting is the vengeance—not the beheading, not the gutting, but the words. And I have so many words— 'chink' words and 'gook' words too—that they do not fit on my skin" (pp. 62–63).

"Winged-words," Ong (1982, p. 77) tells us, suggest evanescence, power, and freedom. The power of Momaday's and Kingston's narratives resides in their imaginative projection of self, which creates a bridge between self and other, between past, present, and future, as well as between spaces. Whether it be Indian reservations or Old China and the United

States, Momaday and Kingston situate themselves at the cultural, communal nexus.

Rodriguez, on the other hand, is hampered by his inability to claim his past. In fact, he celebrates his dissociation from his communal self: "I do not write as a modern-day Wordsworth seeking to intimate the speech of the poor. I sing Ariel's song to celebrate the intimate speech my family once freely exchanged. In singing the praise of my lower-class past, I remind myself of my separation from that past, bring memory to silence. I turn to consider the boy I once was in order, finally, to describe the man I am now. I remember what was so grievously lost to define what was necessarily gained" (p. 6). Rodriguez's stance, like that of Angelou, Momaday, and Kingston, is self-determined and selected. Angelou, Momaday, and Kingston choose to create ideas of themselves that claim communion with their culture; Rodriguez chooses to reject his own. In speaking of the dilemma of choice that presents itself in art, John Gardner (1977, p. 126) believes:

> Real art creates myths a society can live instead of die by, and clearly our society is in need of such myths. What I claim is that such myths are not mere hopeful fairy tales but the products of careful and disciplined thought; that a properly built myth is worthy of belief, at least tentatively; that working at art is a moral act; that a work of art is a moral example. . . . The black abyss stirs a certain fascination, admittedly. . . . But the black abyss is merely life as it is or as it soon may become, and staring at it does nothing, merely confirms that it is there.

According to Gardner's worldview, Rodriguez has given us the black abyss. Angelou, Momaday, and Kingston recognize that the abyss of alienation exists but assert themselves over it, creating new myths to live by. One can say that autobiographies amount to mythologies of the self; in the case of *Hunger of Memory*, the myth is self-selectively destructive. The difference between these other writers and Rodriguez lies in a participatory affirmation of a personal and communal past. The differences create two kinds of images of the self: one that is culturally congruent with the past, and one that is not. When speaking of the difference between visual and oral processes, Ong uses the metaphor of a drum to illustrate his point. One can see a drum from the outside but cannot approximate its interior because it is hidden from view. When the drum is struck, however, sound resonates and, through the character of the sound, conveys the sense of the interior. In this way, Rodriguez describes the exterior of his drum, leaving his interior silent. Angelou walks us around the interior of her drum, while Momaday and Kingston strike their drum, letting the resonance of their interior surround them with sound.

Kingston ends her autobiography with a story about Ts'ai Yen, who was captured by the barbarians and lived with them in exile for many years. One day Ts'ai Yen heard a high, wailing sound outside her tent. Kingston explains that "she walked out of her tent and saw hundreds of the barbarians sitting upon the sand, the sand gold under the moon. Their elbows were raised, and they were blowing on flutes. They reached again and again for a high note, yearning toward a high note, which they found at last and held—an icicle in the desert" (pp. 242–243). Ts'ai Yen counters with her own high, wailing sound. We are told that "her words seemed to be Chinese, but the barbarians understood their sadness and anger" (p. 243). When released from captivity, she brought these songs back with her, and they have been handed down through the generations. One of these is "Eighteen Stanzas for a Barbarian Reed Pipe," a song that Chinese sing to their instruments. Kingston observes that "it translated well."

An autobiography is an attempt to capture and hold the self, as paradoxical and difficult an enterprise as sustaining an icicle in the desert. And for the ethnic American autobiographer, retaining the sense that one is in the land of the barbarians is essential to being able to effect one's song. The song sustains the paradox. Rodriguez has not realized the true value of being in the land of the barbarians; he has forfeited a song. Indeed, in the words of Oliver Goldsmith, "Silence is become his mother tongue."[7]

CHAPTER 4

All the acts of the drama of world history were
performed before a chorus of laughing people.
Without hearing the chorus we cannot understand
the drama as a whole.

M. M. BAKHTIN
Rabelais and His World

Power Reversals
and the Comic

ROLANDO HINOJOSA

AS A POLITICAL WRITER

As noted in previous chapters, social drama is central to understanding the unique oppositional stance that Chicanos pose in their literature. It is a phenomenon based on conflict and underscores the process of confrontation that exists in social situations. Victor Turner has characterized this social tension as an alternation between fixed and floating worlds. People achieve balance by creating "liminal areas of time and space — rituals, carnivals, dramas, and latterly films [that] are open to the play of thought, feeling, and will; in them are generated new models, often fantastic, some of which may have sufficient power and plausibility to replace eventually the force-backed political and jural models that control the center of a society's ongoing life" (Turner 1969, p. vii).

In his fictional Belken County, Rolando Hinojosa creates a liminal space in which social and political power is contested. He sets forth a self-reflexive time and space in which the conflictual dimensions of historical time are played out. Turner (1969, p. vii) explains that in these reflexive types of aesthetic forms the social process itself is represented: "society becomes at once subject and direct object. . . . if we were as dialectical as we claim to be, we would see that it is more a matter of an existential bending back upon ourselves." Life as depicted in Belken County, the characters who appear and the historical events that are recounted, can be said to constitute a subjective "bending back upon ourselves." It represents the agonistic process of social time for Mexicans in South Texas, but, more importantly, it is a dramatistic unraveling that points to social and political change. Through his serial novel the Klail City Death Trip Series, Hinojosa offers a concrete counterworld dramatizing the very plausibility and possibility of the survival of Mexicans (J. Saldívar 1985a; R. Saldívar 1990; Hernández 1989).

Yet the comic form of his narrative seems to belie the gravity of his task. Turner (1969, p. vii) would disagree, however, since "our concreteness, our substantiality is with us in our reflexivity, even in the ludic play domain of certain of our liminal moments: play is more serious than we, the inheritors of Western Platonism, have thought." Because the study of the comic is particularly important to understanding Chicano literature, I will analyze the dialectic of Hinojosa's multiformed play in order to chart the oppositional character of Chicano literature and explore the reflexivity inherent in his work by describing the comic technique he employs. I will first consider traditional comic elements, then analyze the structural use of contradiction, and culminate in a study of carnival in the narrative. This chapter thus unfolds from the specific to the general and offers an ever-widening interpretation of the open comic text that Hinojosa continues to create.

LANGUAGE CONSCIOUSNESS

Perhaps one of the most memorable comic scenes in Rolando Hinojosa's oeuvre depicts the death of Bruno Cano in the sketch "Al pozo con Bruno Cano," in *Estampas del valle y otras obras*.[1] In the great comic tradition, Hinojosa offers an intercalated tale of why the priest, Don Pedro Zamudio, refuses to officiate at the burial of the late Bruno Cano. The tale within a tale is predicated on wordplay, coincidental meetings, and the consequences of language misunderstood.[2] Although the scene is long, analysis of a few sections underscores Hinojosa's use of these elements.

Melitón Burnias and Bruno Cano are searching for buried treasure. Cano is in the hole they have dug when this dialogue ensues:

> ¿Melitón, Melitón, no oíste? Creo que vamos cerca.
> ¿Qué si no oí? ¿Qué si no oí qué?
> Te digo que vamos cerca.
> Ah, sí, pues entonces, ¿qué rezo yo?
> ¿Qué?
> ¿Que qué rezo yo?
> ¿Cómo que qué resolló?
> ¿Qué resolló algo?
> ¿Qué resolló algo dices?
> ¿Qué resolló? ¡ay, Diosito mío!
>
> Diciendo esto, Burnias voló; abandonó la pala y a su socio; empezó a gritar, convencido, tal vez, que un fantasma que resollaba venía por él. (p. 36)

"Melitón! Melitón! Didn't you just hear that? I think we're gettin' close!"

"What was that?"

"Close! I said we're gettin' *close here.*"

"A ghost? Near, did you say?"

"What? What did you say? A ghost? Where-a-ghost? Here?"

"There-a-ghost? Oh, *dear!* My God, my God, it's *clear!*"

"A ghost is clear? Is that what you said, goddamit? Melitón? What are you doing? Melitón! Answer me!"

"A ghost? Bruno, I gotta get outta here!"

"A ghost? Did that idiot . . . Jesus! Did he say a *ghost!* Jesus, save me Lord!"

By this time, Burnias was headed straight for the melon patch and making good time. (p. 38)

Bruno Cano, who has been left in the pit speculating on the possible appearance of a ghost, begins to yell:

¡Sáquenme! ¡Sáquenme de aquí! ¡Qué me matan! ¡Sáquenmeeeeeee! ¡Con una chingada! ¡Ay yay yay, Diosito santo! ¡Qué me saquen! ¡Ayúdenme! (p. 36)

"Help! Heeeeeelp! Help me, goddamit! Sorry, Lord. Je-sus Christ, get me out of here! Help me, help me out there, somebody!" (p. 38)

Ironically, his prayer is heard, and herein lies his fate, for the priest Don Pedro comes to his aid:

¿Qué pasa? ¿Qué hace usted allí?

¿Es usted don Pedro? Soy yo, Cano. Sáqueme.

¿Pues qué anda haciendo Ud. por esta vecindad?

Sáqueme primero. Más al luego le cuento.

¿Se golpeó cuando se cayó?

No me caí . . . ayúdeme.

Sí, hijo, sí; ¿pero entonces como vino a dar allí? ¿Seguro que no está lastimado?

Segurísimo, señor cura, pero sáqueme ya con una . . . perdón.

¿Qué ibas a decir, hijo?

Nada, Padrecito, nada; sáqueme.

No creo que pueda yo sólo; estás muy gordo.

¿Gordo? ¡Gorda su madre!

¿Mi quééééééé?

Sáqueme ya con una chingada. ¡Andele!

¡Pues que lo saque su madre!

¡Chingue la suya!

Don Pedro se persignó, se hincó cerca del pozo, y se
puso a orar aquello de " . . . recoge a este pecador en tu
seno" cuando Bruno Cano le mentó de la madre otra vez.
Tan clarita fue la mentada que hasta los pájaros dejaron de
trinar. (p. 37)

"Who are you? What's going on down there?"

"Is that really you, don Pedro? This is me, Cano. Help
me up, will ya?"

"What are you up to in this part of town?"

"Look, get me out o' here, and then we'll talk, 'kay?"

"Are you all right? Did you injure yourself when you
fell down?"

"What? No, no, I didn't fall down here . . . Come on,
help me up."

"All in good time, all in good time. Now, tell me, how
was it you wound up down there, and are you sure you're
not hurt in some way? I was sure I heard some screa . . ."

(Interruption) "That was me, but I'm okay, really. Now,
for God's sake, hurry up and get me the hell . . . sorry."

"And what was it you were about to say, my son?"
(Knowingly)

"Nothing, Reverend Father, sir—just get me o' this
hole. Please."

"Well, it's this way: I'd like to, but I don't think I can,
you know. I mean, you *are* a little, ah, heavy, ah, a little fat,
you know."

"Fat? Faa-aaaaaat? Your Mama's the fat one!"

"My whaaaaaaaaaaaaaat?"

"Your Mother! That's who! That *Cow*! Now, get me
the hell out o' here! Do it!"

"Speaking of mothers (sweetly), friend Cano, maybe
yours can get you 'out o' that hole'!"

"Why, you pug-nosed, pop-eyed, overripe, overbearing,
overeating, wine-swilling, son-of-a-bitch! You do your
duty as a priest!"

"I will, my son, I will," he purred.

With this, don Pedro knelt at the edge of the hole: First, a rapid sign of the Cross, and skipping the Our Father altogether, don Pedro started on the one about . . . "clasp, o' Lord, this sinner to your breast" and then Bruno let go with another firm reminder of don Pedro's mother. This time, the reminder was as plain as West Texas, and the birds stopped at mid-trill. (p. 39)

The priest continues to pray over the unfortunate Bruno Cano until dawn, first with an entire rosary and then with a complete recitation of the Mass for the dead. He concludes this liturgy of prayer by observing:

¿No ve? Con los rezos se allega a la paz. Ya va amaneciendo. Dentro de poco vendrán por usted.

"Now, do you see? Prayers *do* bring inner peace, don't they? They've stilled your anger, my son, and tempered both our faiths. Rest easy, the sun will soon be coming up, and so will you." (pp. 39–40)

But Bruno Cano has achieved his ultimate peace. In a fit of apoplexy, he dies during the night:

Bruno no le puso cuidado. Ni lo oyó siquiera. Bruno Cano había echado el bofe entre uno de los misterios del rosario y una de las madres. Entregando, así, su alma al Señor, al Diablo, o a su madre; a escoger. (p. 37)

Bruno was past caring. Somewhere just after one of the mysteries or one of Bruno's motherly recollections, Bruno stopped breathing and thus delivered his uneasy soul to the Lord, the devil, or to don Pedro's mother. Or to none of the above. (p. 40)

Eventually, Don Pedro is persuaded to bury Bruno Cano, and the funeral becomes a festival for the town of Flora. Inhabitants from neighboring towns come by the busload for the event, which has achieved great importance in the community. Cano's fellow townspeople set up booths to sell food and drink, and much merriment accompanies the ritual of his passing.

Many of the elements that Northrop Frye attributes to comedy are present in this passage. We have an ethos, or plot, in which a "stable and harmonious order [is] disrupted by folly, obsession, forgetfulness, 'pride' and 'prejudice,' or events not understood by the characters themselves, and then restored" (Frye 1957, p. 171). Moreover, this ethos is complicated, and there is something absurd about the complications (Frye 1957, p. 170). Also, we find the curious doubling of figures, wherein Melitón Burnias and Bruno Cano reflect ambivalent traits and play off against one another in order to advance the mythos as well as the dianoia of the scene. Melitón's cowardice, amplified by Bruno's pride and impatience, has comic/tragic results. But Frye's categorization of mythoi and the various stages of comedy, which would give rise to analysis of the elements mentioned above, leaves much to be desired. I agree with Frank Lentricchia (1980, p. 16) that "Frye's system predisposes the critic not to perceive the freshness of transformation; it has difficulty accounting for individuality in expression, for ruptures and discontinuities; and it refuses without qualification to recognize the constraining and determining effect of nonliterary forces upon the literary universe."

As an entrée into understanding the forms of transformation evident in the scene under discussion here, and in Hinojosa's series as a whole, we should reconsider some of Suzanne Langer's provocative statements on comic rhythm. Langer's ideas are less literary than philosophical and move us toward comprehending those "nonliterary forces" that contribute to the "literary universe." Reconsideration of her philosophical perspective offers a fruitful angle on the transformative power of comedy. Labeling comedy one of the great dramatic forms, she asserts that "human life-feeling is the essence of comedy. It is at once religious and ribald, knowing and defiant, social and freakishly individual . . . the immediate sense of life is the underlying feeling of comedy, and dictates its rhythmically structured unity, that is to say its organic form" (Langer 1953, p. 331). Like many before her, she foregrounds the essence of comedy in the fertility rites and in the celebration of symbols of perpetual rebirth and eternal life. This approach is not new. In fact, what is usually understood as Western comic action has ancient roots in the revels of Roman and Greek rituals.[3]

But Langer's comments go beyond identifying comedy as revelry to understand its philosophical considerations. This perspective leads her to stress the close interrelationship between the comic and the serious that, she asserts, underlies comic rhythm:

> The serious mood is reserved for the tragic stage. Yet comedy may be serious; there is heroic drama, romantic drama, political drama, all in the comic pattern, yet entirely serious; the "history" is usually exalted comedy. It presents an incident in the undying life of a society that

meets good and evil fortunes on countless occasions but never concludes its quest. After the story comes more life, more destiny prepared by the world and the race. (Langer 1953, p. 334)

The comic incident under discussion here clearly expresses that "human life-feeling," that "immediate sense of life," of which Langer speaks. As mentioned earlier, people from throughout the Valley come to participate in the event taking place in Flora. Yet the importance of the community (writ large) is underscored even earlier in the story. After the entire scene between Don Pedro and Cano unfolds and the latter's demise, we learn: "Como es de suponer, no menos de treinta personas habían observado la escena. Habíanse quedado a una respetable distancia mientras uno rezaba y otro maldecía" (p. 37) (As may be supposed, no less than thirty of us witnessed, so to speak, the sunrise tableau, but we'd all kept a respectful distance while the one chanted and the other ranted [p. 40]).

Like a Greek chorus, the people stand as witnesses to the events that later unite them in a celebration of life. They not only witness but also participate in the death of Bruno Cano. Moreover, they become the vehicle through which this unfortunate incident is transformed into an affirmation of life: they perform actions that assure their place within the ranks of the living. A temporary reversal of life over death occurs, at least for this time of festival:

> Al pesar del calorón, el polvo, el empujar, y la multitud agolpada y remolinándose, no hubo mayor desorden: un pleito que otro, sí, pero sin navajas. Lo que sí se contó fueron los que cayeron: hubo no menos de treinta y cuatro desmayados y fue, en fin, un entierro como Dios manda.
>
> El que no asistió fue Melitón Burnias. Como decía después, "Ese día yo andaba ocupadísimo."
>
> La gente casi ni le ponía atención. (p. 38)

> Now, despite the heat, the dust, the pushing, and the shoving, the crowd behaved itself, considering; there were some frayed nerves here and there, and more shouting than necessary and then there were those thirty-four who fainted, but, all in all, it was a first class funeral.
>
> As it turned out, about the only person missing from all this was Melitón Burnias. As he said, days later: "I was quite busy on some personal business, and I was unable to

get away to give Bruno a proper farewell. I, ah, well . . . ah, you know, it . . ."

Almost everyone pretended they had no idea what it was he was mumbling about, and let it go at that. (p. 41)

The narrator takes an indifferent stance to the fate or feelings of Melitón Burnias, which underscores the attitude that "Life goes on," a philosophical perspective acted out by the townspeople.

This attitude, which emphasizes the progression of life, is necessary to comic rhythm, according to Langer (1953, pp. 334–335): "it is implicit in the episodic structure." The comic pattern "is not a complete organic development reaching a foregone, inevitable conclusion"; rather it "is episodic, restoring a lost balance, and implying a new future." Laughter, or humor, holds the episodic structure together because it helps the audience identify with the worldview presented in the comic situation. This emotive response, Langer contends, constitutes one of the dynamic transformative devices in comic rhythm.

Within the category of laughter we would have to place buffo, or laughter elicited from a folk or vulgate base, as well as parody and irony, which arise from a self-conscious relationship to one's environment. In the case of the characters in the pit, Cano, Burnias, and Don Pedro are buffoons who heighten the comic situation, while the narrator contributes the element of irony by the stance he takes in relation to the story and the townspeople of Flora. Langer suggests that all manifestations of humor elicit a feeling of superiority in the spectator. One laughs, snickers, and sneers, she explains, always in an exclusionary relationship to oneself. The situation could be applicable to anyone, but the laughter ensures that, on this occasion, it applies to others. We can argue with this position, but her fundamental view—that this sense of relief and superiority brought out by laughter is central to the serious, self-reflexive dimension of comedy— is significant. The identification of the spectator with the comic situation is useful and is addressed further below.

At this juncture, it must be noted that although laughter is one of the most recognizable aspects of comedy it is not the essence. Langer (1953, p. 350) concludes that the rhythm of "felt life" seems to be the element of artistic importance, that is, "the essential comic feeling, which is the sentient aspect of organic unity, growth, and self preservation." This rhythm, she argues, proceeds from the serious, passes through the humorous, and finally reaches an organic unification of the dialectical opposites of growth and self-preservation.

Hinojosa achieves his rhythm of felt life primarily through the articulation of language, that is, Valley speech and discourse. Language is a vital element of the organic unity created in the Klail City Death Trip Series; it is at the core of the growth and preservation of the Texas Mexican community Hinojosa presents. I agree with José Saldívar, Rosaura Sánchez, and others that this serial novel can best be understood by bringing to bear some of Bakhtin's observations on the dialogic nature of the novel form. Saldívar (1985b, p. 50) notes that "stylistically, Hinojosa uses his dialogical imagination throughout the project to depict a changing historical materialism in South Texas. His numerous characters reveal themselves to us through what Mikhail M. Bakhtin called 'heteroglossia,' that is, discourses peculiar to a variety of stratum of society." According to Bakhtin (1981, p. 426), to be dialogic is to understand that "everything means, is understood, as a part of a greater whole." Similarly, heteroglossia refers to the "primacy of context over text" (1981, p. 428) in the operation of meaning in any discourse. These concepts are complicated and difficult to summarize. Yet the fundamental idea that discourse in the novel must be understood as multiformed and polyphonic and that it is in constant interaction and transformation must be underscored.

In Bakhtin's view, at the center of this transformative power of discourse are the opposing centripetal and centrifugal forces of language that are brought together in the heteroglot utterance. He explains the phenomenon as follows: "Stratification and heteroglossia widen and deepen as long as language is alive and developing. Alongside the centripetal forces, the centrifugal forces of language carry on their uninterrupted work; alongside verbal-ideological centralization and unification, the uninterrupted processes of decentralization and disunification go forward" (Bakhtin 1981, p. 272).

Bakhtin (1981, p. 272) describes this dynamic process as "a contradiction-ridden, tension-filled unity of two embattled tendencies in the life of language." At various stages in the development of artistic discourses, these centripetal forces, which combine to form a unitary or "standard" language, and the centrifugal forces, which resist such centralization, struggle against each other. For example, in the Middle Ages,

> on the stages of local fairs and at buffoon spectacles, the heteroglossia of the clown sounded forth, ridiculing all "languages" and dialects; there [also] developed the literature of the *fabliaux* and *Schwänke* of street songs, folksayings, anecdotes, where there was no language-center at all,

where there was to be found a lively play with the "languages" of poets, scholars, monks, knights and others,
where all "languages" were masks and where no language
could claim to be an authentic, incontestable face.
(Bakhtin 1981, p. 273)

During this time, Bakhtin infers, these folk forms provided a conscious
opposition to the influence exerted by literary language. Bakhtin (1981,
p. 274), then, finds in the comic a "real ideologically saturated 'language
consciousness,' one that participates in actual heteroglossia and multi-
languagedness." Because the comic uses quotidian and rhetorical language,
which, he explains, are the "carriers of the decentralizing tendencies in the
life of language," it is a form uniquely suited to expose the behavior of
discourse in a contradictory and multi-languaged world.

Rolando Hinojosa deliberately invests his fiction with a self-reflexive
"language consciousness," a choice he describes in Anglo-Texas versus
Texas-Mexican political terms:

> As a few of you may know, I was born in the Valley; I was
> nurtured there and educated there both in Mexican and in
> American schools. One language supplanted the other for
> a while, but eventually they balanced each other out. What
> developed from this, among other matters, was an idiosyn-
> cratic vision of the world; an awareness of differences and
> similarities. What I worked on, as far as my life was con-
> cerned, was toward a personal voice which was to become
> my public voice. (Hinojosa in Saldívar 1985a, p. 13)

Later he relates his choice of voice to a representation of the heteroglot
population of the Valley in South Texas:

> And you'll see that idiosyncratic vision I mentioned ear-
> lier, and you'll be able to read the personal and public
> voices as well as the voices of those hundreds of characters
> who populate the works: the fair and the mean, the fools
> and knaves, the heroes and cowards, those who are selfish,
> and those who are full of self-abnegation in a place called
> Belken County, of which I am the sole owner and propri-
> etor. (Hinojosa in Saldívar 1985a, p. 16)

Those personal and public voices are oppositionally placed against the
official languages of South Texas, both English and Spanish. The discourses of Belken County become analogs for the organization of political

and historical contradictions.[4] The effects of Hinojosa's exposition can only be understood in reference to what Langer has called the co-presence of the audience and what Bakhtin has called "active listeners." Bakhtin (1981, pp. 280–281) reminds us that "all rhetorical forms [of which the novel is one] . . . are oriented toward the listener and his answer. . . . Responsive understanding is a fundamental force, one that participates in the formulation of discourse, and it is moreover an *active* understanding, one that discourse senses as resistance or support enriching the discourse."

Rolando Hinojosa has constructed his series with the resistance and support of his listeners in mind. On the level of plot, he depends upon the response of his readers to supply the needed information that he calculatedly secrets and exposes throughout the narrative. On the level of language, he depends upon the reader to supply the necessary "answer" to the utterance.

Returning to Melitón, Bruno, and Don Pedro, we confront the initial problem, the refusal of the priest to bury Cano. This is a very serious transgression for a priest and a betrayal of human sensitivity as well. Yet we discover through the intercalated tale that the problem arises from a curse that reaches beyond the priest's religious duty to his duty as a son. "Hechar la madre" is a curse of such magnitude that it levels all superimposed higher orders of duty and right conduct. The reader knows some transgression of great magnitude will occur, and when Melitón is scared off by a word misunderstood it is clear that the offense will take place on a linguistic level. As soon as Cano takes back his initial curse—"Segurísimo, señor cura, pero sáqueme ya con una . . . perdón" (That was me, but I'm okay, really. Now for God's sake, hurry up and get me the hell . . . sorry)—the reader anticipates the deed and, if privy to Mexican cultural sensitivities, answers Cano's plea for help with a knowing sigh. When Bruno Cano finally curses the priest's mother, the active listener already has anticipated, and therefore participated in, the emotive dynamics of the scene.

Bakhtin (1981, p. 280) explains that "every word is directed toward an *answer* and cannot escape the profound influence of the answering word that it anticipates." The rhetorical play involved in this interactive dialogue is at the heart of Rolando Hinojosa's style as it is displayed in the small scene under discussion here and as it occurs on a larger scale throughout the series.

We could contend, in fact, that this serial novel constitutes an ongoing conversation between the author and his listening audience. The conversation is a device fundamental not only to understanding the structure of Hinojosa's work but also to comprehending the ideological force of his narrative.[5] When considering the Death Trip Series, Bakhtin's question "Should we imagine the work as a rejoinder in a given dialogue, whose style is determined by its interrelationship with other rejoinders in the same dialogue (in the totality of the conversation)?" would have to be answered with a resounding "yes" (Bakhtin 1981, p. 274). Hinojosa's work can best be understood as a truly dialogized style in which he has shaped his own stylistic profile and tone. For this reason, the series can be constituted out of diverse techniques including the classic comic tale, which I have considered here, and the epistolary form, poetry, and detective fiction, which are genres used in the component volumes of the series. They are bound together by an essential comic rhythm that is rooted in an episodic structure and is based on a transformative heteroglot use of language.

As noted before, one aspect of that rhetorical conversation is a cultural identification based on language. For readers in the know, a curse on one's mother will, and appropriately should, have dire effects. Yet the dimensions of the conversation that Hinojosa creates in the entire series are far more complex and can be better understood by assessing his use of Spanish and English. Many other critics have noted that Hinojosa's use of language progresses from exclusive use of Spanish in his early texts, such as *Estampas del valle* and *Generaciones y semblanzas,* to an increasing interplay of Spanish and English, and finally to exclusive use of English in *Rites and Witnesses* and *Partners in Crime.* They have understood this progression to reflect the process of assimilation that envelops the lead protagonists of the series, Rafe Buenrostro and Jehú Malacara.

I suggest, conversely, that on the level of microlanguage Hinojosa also creates a counterassimilation in the Anglo community. On the microlevel, the use of Spanish by Texas Anglos is placed in opposition to the assimilation of Mexicans to Anglo America taking place on the macrolevel in the Valley. The various instances in which Noddy Perkins speaks to Jehú in Spanish or incorporates Spanish epithets into his speech illustrate his acknowledgment of the power residing in language. On the one hand, we understand the exploitation of the population that underlies the friendly attitude, but in an ironic twist we also understand the hold that the Mexican population subtly exerts over those who hold traditional power. A power reversal, although one of influence and subtle effect, nevertheless occurs. Like Noddy Perkins, Texas Mexicans can say that despite their very real assimilation into Anglo America, "it makes no le hace." The effects of this population's lived experience will continue to affect the definition of life in the Valley for all its inhabitants, whether Texas Mexicans or Anglo Texans.

Bakhtin (1981, p. 276) speaks to this type of linguistic interrelatedness when he writes:

> The word, directed toward its object, enters a dialogically agitated and tension-filled environment of alien words, value judgments and accents, weaves in and out of complex interrelationships, merges with some, recoils from others, intersects with yet a third group: and all this may crucially shape discourse, may leave a trace in all its semantic layers, may complicate its expression and influence its entire stylistic profile.

Rolando Hinojosa understands this process to be distinctly ironic. And this irony is a crucial aspect of the comic rhythm he creates in the rhetorical conversation of the Klail City Death Trip Series.

To return to "Al pozo con Bruno Cano," we might consider ourselves to be metaphorically in that pit, engaged in a conversation with Rolando Hinojosa. We are called upon to join the stops and starts, the questions and answers, yet Hinojosa must look on some of these rejoinders, critical assumptions, and speculations with a knowing eye. He tells us, in fact, at the beginning of *Estampas del valle* that "el escritor escribe y trata de hacer lo que puede; eso de explicar es oficio de otra gente. Uno cumple con escribir sin mostrar la oreja" (What follows, more likely as not, is a figment of someone's imagination; the reader is asked to keep this disclaimer in mind. For his part, the compiler stakes no claim of responsibility; he owns and holds the copyright but little else). Whatever we critics might suppose, Hinojosa intimates, "it makes no le hace," as the inhabitants of Belken County might say. And this very ironic stance consistently underlies Hinojosa's comic rhythm, as it also forms the basis of the enduring attraction of his work.

FEELING THE OPPOSITE

In tristia hilaris, in hilaritate tristis.

GIORDANO BRUNO

Hinojosa's comic rhythm in the series as a whole presents some challenging issues for analysis. Kenneth Burke (1966, p. 24) leads us in the right direction when he ponders, in an extended footnote in *Language as Symbolic Action*, on the human being as the "laughing animal." He explains that, "while laughter, like tears, is grounded in the motions of animality, it also

depends upon principles of congruity that are due to conventions or proprieties developed through the resources of symbolicity. It embodies these
norms of congruity in reverse, by their violation within limits, a kind of
'planned incongruity.'" The dialectical interplay between congruity and
incongruity within the comic text is central to understanding the self-
reflexivity to which the preceding section alludes. Yet the self-consciousness
at play goes beyond the ironic observations of the narrator or author.

In order to explore the congruity and incongruity, irony and comedy,
we turn to a very different perspective on the comic.[6] In his monograph
On Humor, Luigi Pirandello distinguishes between comedy and humor. He
proposes that in comedy, laughter arises out of a *"perception of the opposite,"* a process that distances the perceiver from the phenomenon. Conversely, humor arises out of a *"feeling of the opposite"* in which the observer of emotion is transformed into a participant. A. Iliano and D. P.
Testa, in their introduction to the English translation of Pirandello's
monograph, explain the distinction in the following terms: "Humor, . . .
with its 'feeling of the opposite,' touches a deeper base where it is able to
perceive simultaneously the conflicting aspects of every situation: faced
with a comic situation it will perceive its serious side, and vice versa."[7]
This phenomenon depends on a "special activity of reflection," which,
they underscore, is a crucial element in Pirandello's conception of the creative process of humor.

Pirandello's idea carries Suzanne Langer's insistence that the comic represents "human life-feeling" and an "immediate sense of life" to very different conclusions. His qualification provides an explanation for the twist
of perception that occurs when laughter is melded with the serious, at
times, in an uncomfortable relationship. Iliano and Testa explain that "for
Pirandello, humoristic reflection is an impulsive and spontaneous force
which works from within the creative process, disturbing and disrupting
the movement of images by evoking 'an association through contraries,' so
that the 'images, instead of being linked through similarity or juxtaposition, are presented in conflict'" (p. xii). Pirandello puts the situation far
more creatively when he observes that the humoristic temperament is dual,
"like a violin and double bass at the same time" (p. xii).

The incongruity achieved through the "feeling of the opposite" pervades not only the language and structure of a text, that is, its formal elements, but its effect as well. Pirandello argues that "humor needs a highly
spirited, free, spontaneous, and direct movement of language—a movement that can be achieved only when form creates itself anew each time";

in fact, the "inner and peculiarly essential process of humor is one that inevitably *dismantles*, splits, and disrupts" (p. 31). Many times humoristic texts appear to be disorganized and to contain numerous digressions. Yet what is truly occurring here, according to Pirandello, is a decomposition of images that establishes the incongruity necessary for a true humoristic feeling of the opposite. He cautions against superficial judgments about such texts:

> The disorganization, the digressions, and divergencies
> do not derive from the writer's eccentricities or personal
> whim, but are precisely the necessary and inevitable conse-
> quence of the disturbance and disruption which are pro-
> duced in the organizing movement of the images through
> the work of the active reflection, which evokes an associa-
> tion through contraries: in other words, the images, in-
> stead of being linked through similarity and juxtaposition,
> are presented in conflict: each image, each group of images
> evokes and attracts contrary ones, and these naturally di-
> vide the spirit, which, in its restlessness, is obstinately de-
> termined to find or establish the most astonishing rela-
> tionships between these images. (p. 119)

Stung by Benedetto Croce's criticism of these ideas on humor, Pirandello clarifies his thoughts further: "Humor is art . . . which decomposes the image created by an original feeling in order that from this decomposition a contrary emotion may arise and be present" (p. 121).

Pirandello's analysis has provoked strong criticism, and so have many humoristic texts. Rolando Hinojosa has been criticized for the seemingly random and episodic nature of his texts. The decomposition of the images of South Texas society does not produce enough laughter for some, enough seriousness for others. In her analysis of Hinojosa's serial novel, Rosaura Sánchez (1985, p. 76) describes the text and offers the following comments:

> The novel itself consists of a series of sketches, interviews,
> testimonials, monologues and dialogues arranged in the
> first two books within a spiral structure which allows the
> narrators to circle continuously around the same center
> and on one plane, even as the curves increase and decrease
> as more or less information is provided about new or pre-
> viously seen events and characters. But while the first two

books are limited to a view of heterogeneity in the community, the last two books explore the social and class
contradictions in the Valley. It is the fragmentation and
brief "capsule" style of each account reducing different
phases and periods of time to one plane which decon-
textualize events so that the impact of history or social
change on individual lives and on particular social classes
is not evident.

Sánchez's criticism rests on the privileging of texts that portray the contradictions of society and the roots of social ills directly. Yet, despite her
criticism of what she perceives to be the static nature of the early texts,
Sánchez (1985, p. 77) acknowledges an association of images that criticize
society indirectly: "These static sketches, however, are fraught with underlying contradictions; here and there one catches rapid anecdotal references
to cases of oppression and resistance."

I argue that the associations she sees are not anecdotal, but rather aspects of the "planned incongruity" of which Burke speaks and on which
Pirandello elaborates. Viewed under the aegis of linear time, Hinojosa's
novels may be thought to portray history statically; yet when viewed dialectically within the contradiction implied in the "feeling of the opposite,"
history emerges as a process, that is, social change is placed in humoristic critical focus. Through an "association of contraries," Hinojosa
maintains a subtle, yet steely, critical stance toward the history of Mexicans in Belken County. The history emerges not as already distilled into
rhetorical ideologies or interpretations, but rather as seemingly random
lived experience.

Pirandello (1974, p. 144) argues for the importance of setting forth the
background of ordinary events and common details, the "material substance of life," in order to "incite actions and inspire thoughts and feelings
that are contrary to all that harmonious logic of acts and characters created by the ordinary writers." In the art of humor appears the "searching
of the most intimate and minute details—which may appear trivial or vulgar if compared with the idealized syntheses of art in general—and that
search of contrasts and contradictions which is at the basis of the art of
the humorist as opposed to the consistency sought by others" (p. 144).
Whereas Sánchez sees a movement from heterogeneity to contradiction in
the component texts of the serial novel, I argue that contradiction is at the
basis of the structure of the novel as a whole. In fact, as his later novels
move toward direct exposition of social and political oppression, Hinojosa leaves the realm of the truly dialectical and enters the consistency of

ordinary art. He loses the inherent edge of contradiction that propelled his early texts and enters the literary environment where contradictions become "perceptions" and not "feelings" of the opposite. This is not to say that the later novels lack social criticism; rather it says that the use of contradiction is internal to the structure in the early works and external to the structure in the later ones.

Pirandello (1974, p. 134) writes about the differences between these types of texts: "While the sociologist describes social life as it appears from external manifestations, the humorist, armed with his keen intuition, reveals how profoundly different the outer appearances are from what takes place in the inner consciousness." In order to explore the difference, I will analyze a few of the digressions, sketches, and testimonies that appear and reappear in various forms throughout the novel. The presentation of the stabbing of Ernesto Tamez by Baldemar Cordero, which takes place in the premier volume, *Estampas del valle*, serves as an apt entrée into Hinojosa's method.

The following exposition of the events related to the death of Ernesto Tamez is set against the raucously comic death scene of Bruno Cano, which it follows. Tamez's demise is related in a section of *Estampas del valle* called "Por esas cosas que pasan" (Sometimes It Just Happens That Way, That's All). The reader is given the facts of the event in a sole paragraph supposedly extracted from the *Klail City Enterprise-News* (March 15, 1970). We learn that Baldemar Cordero is in jail following a fracas at a local bar. He is accused of fatally stabbing "Arnesto [*sic*] Tamez, also 30, over the affections of one of the 'hostesses' who works there" (p. 92). That we are to be wary of the facts as presented is subtly hinted at by the casual misspelling of the name of the deceased. As we shall see from what follows, the facts do not betray the human drama or pathos of the situation.

The intimate story of the drama is told through several testimonies sworn before legal authorities of Klail City. The first is the deposition by Baldemar Cordero, who readily admits his guilt in the first line:

> No hay que darle vueltas. Yo maté al Ernesto Tamez en la cantina *Aquí me quedo.* No me pida detalles porque ni yo mismo sé como fue. Pero tiene vuelta de hoja el tal Ernesto; lo dejé tieso. (p. 93)

> What can I tell you? The truth's the truth, and there's no dodging it, is there? It's a natural fact: I killed Ernesto Tamez, and I did it right there at the *Aquí me quedo.* And how can I deny it? But don't come asking me for no

details; not just yet, anyway, 'cause I'm not all that sure
just how it did happen—and that's God's truth, and no
one else's, as we say. That's right; Neto Tamez is gone and
like the Bible says: I can see, and I can hear. (p. 57)

The plain fact that Baldemar Cordero killed Ernesto Tamez is elaborated in the ensuing monologue. Cordero begins to piece together what
did happen in the cantina that night, clarifying for himself, and for us,
the murky circumstances surrounding the murder. His tale of the journey from bar to bar, which brought him to the *Aquí me quedo*, is intercalated with reminiscences of previous encounters with Tamez as well as
a genealogical breakdown of the extended Tamez family and their connections, by marriage and reputation, with the rest of the community.
Through this intricate digression, the bad feeling that has been building
between Ernesto and Balde is fully dramatized. Moreover, Beto's inclusion
of Romeo Hinojosa, the attorney handling the deposition, as witness to
Tamez's reputation draws us into the story: "Usted conoció a Tamez,
¿Verdad?" (p. 93) (You knew Tamez, didn't you? What am I saying? Of
course, you did. Remember that time at Félix Champión's place? [p. 57]).[8]
Therefore, we are aware that although Balde and his brother-in-law, Beto
Castañeda, do not seek trouble and actually try to avert confrontations on
that fateful night, the forces propelling them go very deep. Tamez has repeatedly challenged and insulted Balde Cordero's manhood. The final in-
stance provokes Balde to the point where the stabbing becomes a reflexive
answer to a lifelong taunt:

> Beto me dijo después que a él le chisporroteó sangre en el
> brazo y en la cara. Beto también dijo que yo ni pestañé ni
> nada. De mi parte le diré que no oí nada: ni los gritos de
> las viejas, ni el remolino de los mirones que se acercaron.
> Nada. (p. 94)

> Later on I think it was that Beto told me about the blood
> and about how it just jumped out and got on my arms,
> and shirt, 'n face, and all over . . . Beto also said I didn't
> blink an eye or anything; I just stood there, he said. All I
> remember now is that I didn't hear a word; nothing. Not
> the women, or the screaming . . . Nothing; not even the
> guys who came a-running. Nothing. (p. 59)

As in Faulkner's strategy in the exposition of the murder of Joanna Bur-
den in *Light in August*, the emphasis is on the forces that impel the action

and not on the action itself. Like Joe Christmas, when Balde eventually exits the bar, he realizes that he has a knife in his hand. The act has been accomplished before he knows it has begun. "Fíjese que he tratado de acordarme del momento preciso cuando sepulté la navaja en el pecho de aquel baboso y nada. En blanco" (p. 95) (You know I've tried to fix, to set down in my mind, when it was that I buried my knife in that damfool. But I just can't remember . . . I just can't, you know [p. 60]).

The bare facts reported in the *Klail City Enterprise-News* have been unmasked for the human and psychological motives and pain they reveal. The fight did not ensue over the mere attentions of a hostess, but over elements far more complex. The truth is that in the *Aquí me quedo*, which in English means "Here I'll Stay," Ernesto Tamez left his life and Balde Cordero left his future.

But the story does not end here. The next deposition is given by Marta, Balde Cordero's sister. Her intimate language underscores her vulnerable relationship to the dominant Anglo society and to the male-dominant society of the barrio. Through her eyes, Balde emerges as the male responsible for the family since the death of their father. He makes decisions for sister and mother, he ensures that they will survive an emotional and economically trying time. Marta continually insists that she does not know anything. What she does know is that this incident will affect her life for years to come:

> Mamá y yo estamos solas sin Balde pero gracias a Dios que todavía tengo a Beto. Ojalá que los Tamez no vengan a buscarle bulla a él porque entonces sí nos hundimos mamá y yo sin hombre en casa. (p. 98)

> Things are going to get tight around here without Balde, but Ma 'n me we still have Beto here, and . . . My only hope is that the Tamezes don't come looking for Beto 'cause that'll really put us under without a man in the house. (p. 65)

Marta lives under the heavy weight of fear of reprisal in the short term and of destitution in the long term. Her familial and economic well-being and security have been left in the *Aquí me quedo*.

The "truth" of this story is affirmed by the fact that it is given as a legal deposition and that it is attested to by an officer of the court, Romeo Hinojosa. Yet the "truth" about life and death that is at the heart of this tale cannot become clear until it is considered in conjunction with its contrary episode. We have in the death of Bruno Cano and Emilio Tamez an "association of contraries" that invites the reader to make comparisons.

I have already discussed in some detail in the previous section the classic comic elements operating in "Al pozo con Bruno Cano." Yet when viewed in relationship to the Emilio Tamez sequence, aspects of similarity and contrast emerge. Both episodes deal with death, but each presents contrastive elements that, taken together, show a broad interpretation of the issue. They both begin by exposing the important role that chance plays in human affairs: Balde points out the irony that if the Reynas had not caused them to leave the Blue Bar they would not have gone to the *Aquí me quedo* and Tamez would still be alive. Moreover, both episodes begin with a curse and end with its challenge: Balde explains that he is sorry for his actions, but if Tamez were to curse and insult him again, he would have to kill him again. These similarities form the basis for the association between the episodes; the dissimilarities lie in far more substantive areas.

As noted, the actual murder of Tamez is secondary to the forces that produced it, while the action of Cano's death is central to the entire tale. At the same time, death itself is at the core of Tamez's story, while death is an intermediary step to communal interaction in Cano's.

Bruno Cano dies before our very eyes in the intercalated tale. Like the townspeople of Flora, we stood "at a respectable distance" while Cano and the priest Don Zamudio "chanted and ranted." Whether Don Pedro was in any way culpable in the death is of no consequence; we, like the people of Flora, must withhold judgment. We, too, are carried along as the action shifts to the festival that begins during the burial. Here death is presented as a catalyst to communal interaction and identification.

Conversely, the principals in the Tamez episode consider the serious issues and effects of taking a human life. Balde Cordero thinks that "a veces me da miedo que maté a un cristiano. ¡Qué cosas! ¿Verdad?" (p. 94) (I killed a human being. Who'd-a thought it? [p. 58]) Later in his monologue he asserts that "créame, me molesta que haya tenido que matar al Ernesto Tamez. A veces pienso que eso de quitarle la vida al prójimo está de la patada" (p. 95) (I feel bad. I can't say how I'll feel later on, but for now, I do, I feel really bad, you know. That stuff about no use crying over spilt milk and all that, that's just talk, and nothing more. I feel terrible. I killed a . . . and when I think about it, real slow, I feel bad . . . Real bad [p. 61]). In his deposition, Beto Castañeda continually states that "Balde is a good man," and we understand the moral predicament in which a "good man" has been rendered a murderer. Balde exists as a person and not as a social or criminal statistic. He epitomizes the pain, guilt, and regret that hover at the core of human action.

Taken separately, these episodes appear to be merely incongruous at best or to be elements in a fragmented text at worst. Yet, when viewed as an "association of contraries," these scenes operate together to widen the breadth of the comic rhythm of the narrative. The laughter elicited by the Cano episode joins the pathos of the Tamez episode. Pirandello states that Giordano Bruno's maxim "In tristia hilaris, in hilaritate tristis" (Merry in sadness, sad in merriment), which is the epigraph for this section, can be considered the motto of humor itself. With this in mind, Hinojosa's serial novel can be seen as a humoristic text: within the laughter it provokes, we experience a "feeling of the opposite," which informs an ongoing connection between disparate elements of the entire narrative. This phenomenon helps us better understand the type of dialogic novel that Hinojosa is creating in the Klail City Death Trip Series.

THE FEAST OF TIME

Carnival was the true feast of time,
the feast of becoming, change and renewal.

BAKHTIN,
Rabelais and His World

The contention that Hinojosa's work is patterned on a type of "planned incongruity," which leads to a decomposition of quotidian images of life in Belken County, and that this imagistic dismantling serves to sustain an "association of contraries" only begins to describe the humoristic technique evident in the Klail City Death Trip Series. To characterize the comic celebration of life in the series involves understanding how Hinojosa's narrative, as a whole, marks the process of death and rebirth that is at the core of lived experience and thus central to sustaining human values.

I have already noted in the previous sections that Hinojosa creates a novel best described in Bakhtin's terms as polyphonic (using a polyphony of voices) and as heteroglot (using a multiplicity of discursive styles). Bakhtin's notions are useful for understanding Hinojosa's work because they emphasize the creative power of language in novel discourse. Bakhtin (1984, p. ix) describes the novel as "the word constantly reinvolved in a dialogue." In her foreword to *Rabelais and His World* (1984, p. ix), Krystyna Pomorska concludes that "behind each reply in this dialogue stands a 'speaking man,' and therefore the word in the novel is always socially charged and thus necessarily polemical. There is no one-voiced novel, and, consequently, every novel by its very nature is polemical." Moreover, language conveys a system of values that is always in conflict, always in a process of formulation and regeneration.

For this reason, Bakhtin's extensive study of carnival in the classic comedy of Rabelais and his later analysis of this term in relation to novel discourse as a whole are of primary importance. Carnival, which originates in folk culture, is predicated on heteroglossia and proceeds under a multiplicity of styles. In this sense, carnival, Pomorska (Bakhtin 1984, p. x) affirms, "is indeed a part of the novelistic principle itself." Furthermore, she explains: "One may say that just as dialogization is the *sine qua non* for the novel structure, so carnivalization is the condition for the ultimate 'structure of life' that is formed by 'behavior and cognition.' Since the novel represents the very essence of life, it includes the carnivalesque in its properly transformed shape."

But the "structure of life," conceived in Bakhtin's perspective, is based on his view that certain forms of art and discourse function to underscore two fundamentally different worldviews—the official and the unofficial. The former proceeds from the all-encompassing dominant authority, while the latter affirms opposition and constitutes a form of authority of the people over the state. Thus, novel structures that are conceived as dialogic are opposed to the "authoritarian word" or "official language" in the same way that carnival is opposed to "official culture." According to Michael Holquist's prologue (Bakhtin 1984, p. xvi), this inherent opposition constitutes a dialectic between "stasis imposed from above and a desire for change from below, between old and new, official and unofficial." The novel thus constituted is an open form that epitomizes a process of continual opposition and regeneration.

Bakhtin's study of carnival in *Rabelais and His World* is an elaborate dissertation in which he charts the process of historical and political change at the center of the transition from the Middle Ages to the Renaissance. The findings of this specific study are, however, more broadly applied in his later work *The Dialogic Imagination* (1981). The folk become a metaphor for unofficial culture, and their laughter, fresh and spontaneous, is at the core of their creative force. Carnival laughter, Bakhtin (1984, p. 88) explains, "builds its own world versus the official world, its own church versus the official church, its own state versus the official state." So conceived, laughter is essential to freedom. Bakhtin describes a comic matrix, at the center of which is a transformative process of regeneration. Although the origin of the matrix reaches back to medieval times and before, the paradigm itself, he demonstrates, is applicable to contemporary texts as well.

The basis of this matrix is the folk, viewed in all their particularity. Bakhtin was drawn initially to the visceral, physical representation of the folk that he found in Rabelais. From this observation, he fashioned an argument about how and why the relations among body, language, and political activity were changing in that historical period. The myriad bodily processes of the folk are placed in imagistic opposition to the restraints of official and social political practice. In the Klail City Death Trip Series, the physicality of the folk is similarly placed in direct opposition to the official culture's expectations of beauty and consistency. Consequently, it is significant that Hinojosa prefaces his premier volume, *Estampas del valle*, with the following declaration:

> Estas estampas son y están como las greñas de Mencho Saldaña: unas cortas, otras largas y todas embadurnadas con esa grasa humana que las junta y las separa sin permiso de nadie. (p. 15)

> The etchings, sketches, engravings, et alii that follow resemble Mencho Saldaña's hair: the damn thing's disheveled, oily, and, as one would expect, matted beyond redemption and relief. (p. 10)

Mencho Saldaña's hair is a metonym for the folk who appear in Hinojosa's serial novel. They are, like the sketches that present them to us, short and long and covered by the human grease that binds and separates them, not by anyone else's command, but by their own inner force. We infer from the authoritative "sin permiso de nadie" (without anyone's permission) that Hinojosa's folk refuse to be dictated to and, above all, to be socially sanitized. This is clearly a folk consciousness of opposition.

As already noted, opposition is central to the force of carnival. Bakhtin traces the history of carnival through premedieval, medieval, and Renaissance times, emphasizing its relation to unofficial culture. The revels, spectacle, and comic theater produced a people's "second life, organized on the basis of laughter . . . a festive life" (1984, p. 8). Most importantly, carnival was always associated with "moments of crisis, of breaking points in the cycle of nature or in the society and man. Moments of death and revival, of change and renewal, always led to a festive perception of the world" (1984, p. 9).

Hinojosa brings this "festive perception of the world" to us in the Klail City Death Trip Series. Through the unofficial culture of the folk of Belken County, he charts a historic moment of crisis in which the Valley itself is dying and a new society is being born. The moment in which birth and death come together is a classic comedic module of historic and festive time. And consideration of its dimensions, its effects, and its results elicits laughter and sadness at the same time. Bakhtin (1984, p. 11) explains the phenomenon as follows:

> All the symbols of the carnival idiom are filled with this pathos of change and renewal, with the sense of the gay relativity of prevailing truths and authorities. We find here a characteristic logic, the peculiar logic of the "inside out" (à l'envers), of the "turnabout," of a continual shifting from top to bottom, from front to rear, of numerous parodies and travesties, humiliations, profanations, comic crownings, and uncrownings. A second life, a second world of folk culture is thus constructed; it is to a certain extent a parody of the extracarnival life, a "world inside out."

It is significant, therefore, that the orphan Jehú Malacara is adopted by Don Víctor Peláez and becomes an apprentice in his circus. From Peláez, Jehú learns the carnival profession and emerges from this early education as one of the leading characters and narrators in the chronicle of Belken County. Jehú's life has been turned "inside out," and through his eyes we see the social and political life of Belken County from the "inside out." Jehú's life incorporates the journey into the interior of social life in the Valley. From performing under the carnival tent, Jehú moves into performing of another sort. In the banking profession, where he becomes enmeshed in the inner workings of the KBC (Klail, Blanchard, Cooke) Enterprise, which cheated, took advantage of, and robbed many Valley Mexicans, Jehú continues to learn about the perennial dynamics of injustice and necessity for survival, which he began to learn under the tutelage of Don Víctor. The old man tells him:

> "Ya párale con eso. Esta noche te trepas aquí en la plataforma y das dos o tres saltos mortales mientras Camilo hace la perorata. Tienes talento, chico, y no hay que desperdiciarlo."
> "¿Usté cree?"
> "No lo dudes. Ahora vamos con lo de la carpa otra vez

y luego a buscarnos unas botellas vacías para la marimba de Leocadio." . . .

Leocadio Tovar (en las tablas Don Chon) soplaba la trompeta y el trombón, y tocaba la marimba de botellas con más ganas que talento. A veces donde falta una cosa hay que suplirle con otra. Ni modo. (pp. 26–27)

"Hold it, Jehú, that's enough. Now, this evening, you just get on that little stool there, jump up and down on one leg, do a somersault or two and watch Camilo go through the routine again. You got talent, kid; let's not waste it."

"You like it, eh?"

"Absolutely. Let's go check those posts and chains again; after that, let's see if we can come up with some empty beer bottles for Leocadio's marimba." . . .

Leocadio Tovar (on the stage: don Chon) huffed and puffed in the brass section, but when it came to playing the marimba . . . he had decided long ago that talent would never get in the way of gusto. And, of course, his never did. (p. 26)

Luckily, the orphaned Jehú has a talent for adapting himself to whatever is required of him, yet Leocadio, who does not have talent, also gets well along in the world. As we are told, you make up for a lack of talent with other things. Jehú's and Leocadio's inventive capacities bind them together and allow them to survive in the lives they are dealt.

Jehú's life is continually changed through death. His parents die, he joins a circus, and then his adopted father, Don Víctor, dies. Jehú explains his reaction to Don Víctor's death: "El día siguiente la Carpa Peláez hizo los preparativos para irse rumbo a Ruffing y yo decidí quedarme en Flora; otra vez la muerte, otra vez huérfano y nuevamente al pairo" (p. 32) (The next day, the Peláez Tent Show loaded up and pointed toward Ruffing, but I decided to stay there, in Flora; Death again, orphaned again, and again lying to with sails set [p. 33]). Just as death plagues the life of the protagonist, death pervades and punctuates the collective life of the people of Belken County. It can be argued that death is the nexus of Belken County life, the pivotal point from which all change is charted.

José Saldívar (1985a, p. 53) believes that the cantinas (bars) that recur in the narrative are "(what Mikhail M. Bakhtin would certainly call a 'chronotopic' patriarchal center in the novel, 'where the knots of narrative are tied and untied')."[9] I suggest that on a broader level the recurrent

death scenes constitute a controlling chronotope that defines the nature of
change and renewal in Belken County life. I have already discussed the incidents of the deaths of Bruno Cano and Ernesto Tamez. I could add the
associated deaths of Pepe Vielma and Esteban Echevarría. The demise of
these two individuals forms opposite poles of the chronotope since they
represent the death of society in micro- and macroscopic terms.

Pepe Vielma, a contemporary of Rafe Buenrostro and a member of the
new generation in the Valley, is killed in the war in Korea. His passing can
be seen as a part of a larger pattern of life and death in the series. In fact,
the Korean conflict pervades the component texts of the series and can be
considered a chronotope for ritualized death and survival that takes place
on global terms. Hinojosa devotes one whole volume, *Korean Love Songs*,
to this chronotope and also interjects the conflict directly into narratives
dealing with the Valley. A continuous contextualization of life and death
is achieved through the narrative interplay of scenes from Korea and the
Valley. Whether Rafe Buenrostro, a soldier in the conflict, will live or die
becomes a tension parallel to the death of the elders and of the old ways in
the Valley. Rafe returns, a survivor of the war; Pepe Vielma, his longtime
friend and neighbor, does not. On returning, Rafe asks, "Le pregunté a Israel que cómo estaban los Vielma. Que bien, que algo tristes de primero
por la muerte de Pepe y que si nunca se conformaron, a lo menos se resig-
naron" (I asked Israel how the Vielmas had taken Pepe's death. They took
it well enough, he said; they'd never get over it, but at least they were re-
signed to it [1986, pp. 186–187]). Both Rafe and the Vielmas must resign
themselves to the incongruity of a Valley Mexican losing his life in a foreign land, for a country in which they are considered alien foreigners. Rafe
recalls:

> Pepe Vielma. Aquí se me hace difícil recordarlo o nom-
> brarle de otra manera; en el ejército, no. Esa fue todavía
> otra vida y allí Pepe Vielma era Joey Vielma; el Joey Vee
> que conocía partes de Kobe y de Nagoya mejor que nadie;
> él, que había leído de todo. Joey Vee: "That two gun's
> firing short; bring it up two clicks." Y cuando nos embor-
> rachamos con el capellán aquella vez, ese también era Joey
> Vee. El muerto no; el muerto era Pepe Vielma.
>
> Pepe Vielma. It's hard to name him, to remember him.
> The army was another life, though. And there, Pepe
> Vielma was Joey Vielma; the Joey Vee who knew parts of
> Kobe and Nagoya better than anyone; he, who had read

just about everything. Joey Vee: "that two gun's firing short, bring it up two clicks." And the time we got drunk with the chaplain, that, too, was Joey Vee. Not the dead man, however; the dead man was Pepe Vielma. (1986, pp. 188–189)

Pepe Vielma, like Rafe and Jehú, is a transitional figure whose life spans Anglo American and Mexican societies as well as the spaces of Belken County and the world. Out there Pepe is Joey Vee, but in death he reverts to his essential Mexicanness indicated by his Spanish name, Pepe Vielma. Pepe's death awakens the association between the new and the old order in the consciousness of Rafe Buenrostro: "Le conté lo de la parranda en el cementerio militar . . . luego le pedí las llaves: 'Voy a ver a Esteban'" (I told him about the wake at the military cemetery, and then I asked him for the keys: "I'm going to see Esteban" [1986, pp. 188–189]). Esteban Echevarría is one of the elders of Belken County, a founding member of the community who carries within his consciousness the origins of Valley culture in Mexican revolutionary lore. He, like Pepe, is destined to pass.

When Echevarría dies, the old idyllic order of the Valley dies too. His stories of the revolution, of the founding of Belken County, are internalized by the new generation. Rafe and Jehú become the next chroniclers of this history, which, it is inferred, might die out as well:

> Echevarría no necesita ser miembro de las Cuatro Familias; ha sobrevivido a todos los de su edad y ahora es el único que todavía se acuerda de cómo era el Valle. De cómo fue y de cómo era el Valle antes de que vinieran los bolillos a montón, y el ejército, el gobierno estatal y sus rinches, el papelaje y "todo el desmadre que arrambló con tierras y familias; con el desprendimiento personal y el honor de haber sido lo que fuimos . . ." Sí; piensa morir. Quizá dure dos, tres días, de ahí no pasa.

> Echevarría does not need to belong to the Four Families, he has survived everyone from his generation and now he is the only one who still remembers how the Valley used to be. How the Valley had been and how it used to be before the Anglos came in herds, before the army, the state government and its rangers, all the bureaucratic paper-work and "all the excesses that swept away lands and families; along with personal generosity and the honor

of having been whom we'd been . . . " Yes; he's planning to
die. He'll die in two, three days, no more than that. (1986,
pp. 128–129)

Echevarría laughs when he recalls Jehú's words: "lo que más siento son
las maldiciones que Echevarría se ha de llevar cuando se muera" (what I
regret the most is the cussing and the swearing that Echevarría is going to
take with him when he dies [pp. 130–131]). Jehú and Rafe will miss the old
man's oppositional voice, which Hinojosa has strategically placed against
the loss of the Valley's Mexican character. In fact, Echevarría's last extended monologue, "Con el pie en el estribo" (Going West), is a digressive
lamentation on the death of the Mexican Valley: "Casas sin corredores,
calles sin faroles, amigos que mueren, jóvenes que ya no hablan español
ni saben saludar . . . ¡Je! Desaparece el Valle, gentes" (Houses without
porches, streets without lamp lights, friends who've died away, and the
youngsters who no longer speak Spanish, who can't even say, "¿Cómo
está?" ¡Hah! The Valley's no longer the Valley, folks [1986, pp. 206–207]).
Echevarría leaves the future of the Valley to Rafe and Jehú, who still
speak the Spanish language, who are university educated, and who have a
knowledge and experience of the world outside Belken County. To them is
entrusted the process of death and renewal, the process incorporating
change.

It is significant, then, that Hinojosa dedicates the next volume in the series, *Partners in Crime,* to solving a homicide. Rafe Buenrostro, now a police
detective, must determine who are the culprits in a tale involving murder,
drugs, and corruption in the Valley. He must ferret out the truth and
reestablish a harmonious order. Placed in its rightful context, opposite the
ruminations on death in the Valley chronicled repeatedly in *Rites and Witnesses, Dear Rafe,* and *Claros varones de Belken,* this novel, in the detective genre,
emerges as a brilliant figure for the reversal of death and affirmation of life
in the Valley.

Through the passing of Bruno Cano, Ernesto Tamez, Pepe Vielma, and
Esteban Echevarría, death and renewal are uncovered as the nexus of Belken County life. In the classic comic sense, the community derives merriment in the festival that accompanies Cano's funeral, but the recounting of
the circumstances surrounding the death of Ernesto Tamez adds the intimate story of passion that impels events. Thus, Hinojosa removes the
carnivalesque mask a little at a time. He exposes little by little the social
dynamic at the root of the Cano episode. Cano's greed leads him to exca-
vate for treasure and ultimately brings his death. Greed, we finally under-

stand through Echevarría, is at the heart of the death of Mexican Valley culture. Through an "association of contraries," these incidents open Valley culture from the "inside out." Hinojosa has created a comic matrix, a "second world of folk culture," in which death becomes the preliminary stage for cultural regeneration.

The most recent novels deal directly with the dying of the culture, and in the larger sense they indicate the dying of laughter as the regenerative force in Valley life. But through the detective genre, and through his transitional narrator, Rafe Buenrostro, Hinojosa begins to reestablish order. We begin to see regenerative powers in other figures as well. Viola Barragán, for example, comes face to face with death, so to speak, while having intercourse: her partner dies of a heart attack, but she lives on. Her life force is sexual as well as entrepreneurial and bodes well for the future of Mexicans in the Valley.[10] The image of death and life coming together in the procreative act is tremendously comic and emblematic of the carnivalesque chronotope found in Hinojosa's serial novel. Each text, or each scene in the series of volumes, may not be comic in the traditional sense, but when they are viewed together as aspects of an open text in which contrary elements of laughter and pain emerge Hinojosa's project becomes a humoristic exploration of the ever-present contradictions and contraries of life.

Victor Turner (1981, pp. 162–163) would add that Hinojosa's decomposition of Valley culture is positive because "dismembering may be a prelude to remembering, which is not merely restoring some past intact but setting it in living relationship to the present." Thus, Hinojosa continues to create a vehicle through which he inscribes himself into history. Clearly, the Klail City Death Trip Series is a "true feast of time, the feast of becoming, change, and renewal."

As a positive, carnivalesque celebration of the process of becoming, Hinojosa's "feast of time" is an appropriate image for the future of Chicano literature, because the indeterminacy of the process is essential to discovering creative strategies of survival. Turner (1981, p. 164) comments that "where historical life itself fails to make cultural sense in terms that formerly held good, narrative and cultural drama may have the task of *poesis*, that is, of remaking cultural sense, even when they seem to be dismantling ancient edifices of meaning that can no longer redress our modern 'dramas of living.'" As part of this volume's attempt to explore the ways in which Chicanos are remaking cultural sense for themselves, this chapter focuses on the regenerative power of laughter. Italo Calvino (1982, p. 70) has written that "only laughter . . . can guarantee that our words match up to the terribleness of living and mark a truly revolutionary mutation in us." Hinojosa's comic novel of process underscores the beauty and terribleness of living and, as such, foregrounds the truly revolutionary contribution of Chicano literature as a whole.

CHAPTER 5

To survive the Borderlands
you must live *sin fronteras*
be a crossroads.

GLORIA ANZALDÚA
"To Live in the Borderlands Means You"

I live in a doorway
between two rooms . . .

PAT MORA
"Sonrisas"

Engendering the Border

TOWARD A CHICANA

LITERARY AESTHETIC

THE BORDER

The border between Mexico and the United States has been a contested locale. Américo Paredes (1979, p. x) alludes to the unique quality of this contestation: "every Mexican knows that there are two Mexicos, just as he knows that there being two is not a purely metaphysical concept, although it has its transcendental implications." We critics of the literature written by Mexicans in the United States have tended to underscore the importance of the political and social conflict of the region in the development of our literature and to give less attention to those "transcendental implications" of which Paredes speaks. Yet the Southwest was inhabited by Mexicans and Indians for centuries before Anglo Americans entered this land, and this fact is vitally significant to understand why Mexicans have fought so tenaciously to retain cultural as well as political governance and to assess why the roots of Mexican identity in the territory are so deep.

The border may imply separations, divisions, and culturally discrete boundaries on the one hand, but on the other it negates the possibility of separation and affirms a fluidity of movement. The border is an area that stands geographically, as well as politically and culturally, as figure and metaphor for the transition between nations and for the complex connections that continue to exist for all Mexicans, whether border residents or not. In its transcendent form, the border is a figure of permanence and change; it has become a metaphor that underscores the dialectical tension between cultures, a tension that forms the core identity of the region, a people, and their literature. Yet the metaphor appears to belie the central issue of jeopardy: at stake here is the very survival of a people. Given this larger importance, Carey McWilliams's prophetic final words to *North from Mexico* suggest an even wider global signifying designation and must be reinvoked here. Commenting on the use of the territory to spawn the

atomic bomb, he concludes: "Here in the heart of the old Spanish borderlands, the oldest settled portion of the United States, a new world has
been born and the isolation of the region has been forever destroyed. Like
the peoples of the world, the peoples of the borderlands will either face
the future 'one and together' or they are likely to find themselves siftings
on siftings in oblivion" (McWilliams 1968, p. 304).

The threat of oblivion applies to us all. It can become a metaphysical
question, a spiritual opportunity for affirmation, or a cultural cry of indeterminacy. For most Chicano male writers of the protest decades, the response to the threat of oblivion was to establish a "sense of place," a physical referent whose roots lie in the political struggle for survival in this
land. Rolando Hinojosa invents Belken County as an analog to the historical, political, and cultural life of the Valley in South Texas. Rudolfo
Anaya memorializes the spiritual quality of the struggle by archetypal reference to the land in *The Silence of the Llano*. Tomás Rivera intimates the transcendental quality of the border in his *Y no se lo tragó la tierra* when he writes
about that disembodied litany of voices who lament, "Cuando lleguemos"
(When we arrive). The migrant workers voice the indeterminacy of their
lives, and by doing so point to that middle space to which we all must assign meaning.

For Guillermo Gómez-Peña (1988, p. 130), performance artist, playwright, and cultural critic, the threat of oblivion is not nuclear but cultural, and this sensibility is central to the gestalt of the border:

> The demographic facts are staggering: The Middle East
> and Black Africa are already in Europe, and Latin Amer-
> ica's heart now beats in the U.S. New York and Paris in-
> creasingly resemble Mexico City and São Paulo. Cities like
> Tijuana and Los Angeles, once socio-urban aberrations,
> are becoming models of a new hybrid culture, full of un-
> certainty and vitality. And border youth—the fearsome
> "cholo-punks," children of the chasm that is opening be-
> tween the "first" and the "third" worlds, become the in-
> disputable heirs to a new *mestizaje* (the fusion of Amer-
> indian, African, and European races).
>
> In this context, concepts like "high culture," "ethnic
> purity," "cultural identity," "beauty," and "fine arts" are
> absurdities and anachronisms. Like it or not, we are at-
> tending the funeral of modernity and the birth of a new
> culture.

That new culture repudiates both a monocultural and a binary existence. Instead it affirms the creative force of cultural multiplicity. As an aspect of this fluid culture, a new discourse is in the making, a "border semiotics" based on an articulation of multiple repertories. Gómez-Peña (1988, pp. 127–128) takes the geopolitical space of the border between Mexico and the United States, a place he calls "the fissure between two worlds, the infected wound," and expands it into possible "alternative cartographies" constructed out of the "rubble of the Tower of Babble of our American post-modernity." Here the artistic product results from hybrid and conflicting realities and is composed within a new discourse predicated on contradiction. This artistic space affirms geopolitical interconnections (Latin America and Chicanos, Africa and African Americans), and it is fertile ground, so to speak, for new "options in social, sexual, spiritual, and aesthetic behavior." Gómez-Peña (1988, p. 130) calls himself a "cultural cartographer, border crosser, and hunter of myths." As an artist, he sees his role within this artistic space as emerging from an "epistemology of multiplicity" and his discourse as drawing from contradictions and ambiguities that take root in border spaces. For Gómez-Peña, this is the web of consciousness that emerges from living and creating in the borderlands.

For many contemporary Chicana writers, the border, although rooted in place, evolves into a form of signifying space. Julia Kristeva's thoughts on the formation of "women's time," although controversial, are suggestive for understanding Chicana writing because she points to a process of symbolic designation in which a nexus of body, sex, and symbol comes together to inscribe moments of historical/political action: " 'Father's time, mother's species,' as Joyce put it; and, indeed, when evoking the name and destiny of women, one thinks more of the space generating and forming human species than of *time*, becoming, or history" (Kristeva 1981, p. 33).[1] In other words, for Kristeva, when women are thought of, it is in reference to the space or function of our birthing capacity—a point of orientation for all individuals—origin, mother. Whereas when men are thought of, it is in reference to global movements of time, to history. Linear time, Kristeva believes, is masculine, civilizational, and obsessional, while fundamental temporality is female, extra subjective, and cosmic.

Moreover, Kristeva envisions this process occurring in what she calls a sociocultural ensemble based upon a "symbolic denominator" that is a nexus of body, sex, and symbol. These elements comprise a dynamic in which various kinds of time operate. She borrows Friedrich Nietzsche's ideas by positing both cursive (that is, the time of linear history) and monumental time (which "englobes the supranational") and links the sociocultural ensembles within even larger entities. In this way, Kristeva allows the notion of time to supersede national, cultural constraints and to become a liberating connecting force. She explains that "the question is one of sociocultural groups, that is, groups defined according to their place in production, but especially according to their role in the mode of reproduction and its representations which, while bearing the specific sociocultural traits of the formation in question, are *diagonal* to it and connect it to other sociocultural formations" (Kristeva 1981, pp. 32–33).

Although I will not entertain Kristeva's complex ideas in depth here, I do want to mention her belief that in our symbol-making both kinds of time can—and must—merge, interweaving history and geography, time and space, masculine and feminine. All these dualities I have mentioned are contained in this process. Women's writing lies within the synthesis and contradictions of these dualities as they evolve and as they constitute an expanded notion of "space," "time," and "voice." This process begins in the arena of the immediately personal but extends out toward supranational connections.

What Kristeva comments on theoretically, Tey Diana Rebolledo begins to work out critically in her analysis of Chicana writers' moment of renaming the land in their image. Although in her 1989 article "Tradition and Mythology: Signatures of Landscape in Chicana Literature" Rebolledo couches her analysis in traditional theories of the aesthetics of landscape, her theoretical assumptions are far more complex than mere thematic commentary. In her analysis of Denise Chávez's work, she illuminates a symbolic designation that she sees operating in much of contemporary Chicana writing: "The sexuality of the landscape seen as female, the female body, female response stand as a central metaphor for union, integration of woman, land, and man. The landscape becomes for Chávez an all-surrounding female force" (Rebolledo 1989, p. 118). Although landscape too often connotes a static reference point for writers, Rebolledo affirms landscape as an active inscription of self for Chicanas. The process of becoming, naming, and claiming the self occurs in this signifying moment in which the land itself is transcended. The writers I consider here revel in the literary and political possibilities of this indeterminate space, which we call the "border," and affirm for themselves a personal/political dialectic of claiming and naming for themselves and their communities, whatever they might conceive them to be.

Gloria Anzaldúa, in her *Borderlands/La Frontera*, comments on the creative, albeit painful, possibility of the border:

The U.S.-Mexican border *es una herida abierta* where the Third World grates against the first and bleeds. And before a scab forms it hemorrhages again, the lifeblood of two worlds merging to form a third country—a border culture. Borders are set up to define the places that are safe and unsafe, to distinguish *us* from *them*. A border is a dividing line, a narrow strip along a steep edge. A borderland is a vague and undetermined place created by the emotional residue of an unnatural boundary. It is in a constant state of transition. (Anzaldúa 1987, p. 3)

In this "vague and undetermined space," Chicanas locate and inscribe themselves within the larger political location of the "we" and "them"; that opposition may be conceived of as race, class, gender, or all three. It is a space in which history and women's time coalesce and produce the creative power of women's voice. The border is a crucible where sex, symbol, life, and death play major roles. It is a place of symbolic designation in which the voice of women's literature expands as it enters history, and, in a counterprocess, history itself is changed by this voice within it. This evolution of women's time has been and is essential to producing a women's voice, a process that, Kristeva suggests, is played out in generations of women's thought.

GENERATIONS OF WOMEN'S THOUGHT: BORDER ACTIVISM

Generations in Chicana discourse and thought demand closer reconsideration: the dynamic evolution of the contemporary Chicana voice has not, to date, been adequately placed into the narrative of traditional Chicano history. Chicana activism of the protest decades has clearly produced an increasingly insistent voice and feminist presence that have fostered many contemporary writers. Yet this presence does not begin in this era; rather it is linked to several precursor moments in which women's political action and personal voice have intersected.

In the few analyses published about the Chicano Student Movement, only rarely does the contribution of women emerge as part of the historical record, although women have been and continue to be at the core of political activity. During the years I was involved in student organizations (1967–1980), including MASC (Mexican American Student Committee),

UMAS (United Mexican American Students), and MECHA (Movimiento Estudiantil Chicano de Aztlán), women comprised at least half, and often more, of the membership; these women stood in picket lines, were arrested, mailed newsletters, recruited students, raised bail money, and supported strikes. Women participated in central UMAS and attended EICC (Educational Issues Coordinating Committee) meetings, as well as those of groups such as Black Student Union and LUCHA. These are the political actions that defined the nature of student activism at the time. This is not to say that women did not hold office or exert leadership. They consistently did so throughout the years. We only have to turn to women such as Ana Nieto Gómez, Evelyn Márquez, Adelaida del Castillo, Elsa Iris García Escríbano, and Isabel Rodríguez in California, Betita Martínez in New Mexico, and Blandina Cárdenas Ramírez in Texas. These women claimed wide networks on campuses, in various communities, and in organizations. Their activism continually challenged the definition and scope of Chicano politics.

But the political participation by women has a larger significance. Kristeva (1981, p. 51), when she speaks of "generations" of women's thought, "implies less a chronology than a *signifying space*"; that is, she points to moments in which the definition of the subject is iterated. To use her terminology, these moments of signifying space for Chicana writers occur, for the most part, in relationship to Chicano politics. As we know, Chicano history has been characterized by struggle, both within the group to define itself and outside the group to ensure its own survival. The contradictory nature of this struggle has been and is exacerbated by women defining themselves at times in tandem with and at times in opposition to the overall struggle. The evolving definition of a women's "voice" has meant a painful and meticulous self-criticism including one's class relationship to an increasingly heterogeneous community. The contradictions that arise are enormous and continue to infuse the debate about political struggle for Chicanos. Let us consider two tandem voices that profile the continuity of women's time through significant "generations of thought."

Perhaps the most instructive of these moments occurred in the years prior to the Mexican Revolution and the overthrow of the dictatorship of Porfirio Díaz. The activities and writings of Sara Estela Ramírez document her participation in the Partido Liberal Mexicano, an anarchist political party headed by Ricardo Flores Magón and his brother that conducted its revolutionary activities, for the most part, in exile in the United States. Emilio Zamora, who was one of the first to assess the importance of Ramírez as a political and literary figure in his article "Sara Estela

Ramírez: Una rosa roja en el movimiento," explains that although she was born in the Mexican state of Coahuila she came to Laredo, Texas, in 1898: "During the twelve years that she lived in Laredo, Ramírez was notable for her literary activity in local Spanish language newspapers and for her political association with the Partido Liberal Mexicano (PLM). Many of her political writings are philosophical contributions to PLM activities and, by extension, to the Mexicano socio-political movement of South Texas" (Zamora 1980, p. 163). Zamora documents her role as close advisor to the leaders of the PLM and also as mentor to other women through her writings.

The development of a feminist perspective was central to the PLM project. In fact, it published a manifesto, "A la mujer," that characterizes the coming revolution as a female who carries within her the possibility for change: "Let us welcome her with serenity, for although she carries death in her breast, she is the announcement of life, the herald of hope. She will destroy and create at the same time; she will raze and rebuild. Her fists are the invincible fists of a people in rebellion. She does not offer roses or caresses; she offers an axe and a torch" (Magón 1980, p. 160). The future is in the hands of women as they are called upon to promote social transformation: "men and women alike [are] suffering the tyranny of a political and social environment in complete discord with the progress of civilization and the advances of philosophy" (p. 162).

Sara Estela Ramírez arises from this affirmation of the power of women to transform society. All of her activities are marked by this understanding. Her journalistic contributions to *La Crónica* and *El Demócrata Fronterizo,* her publication of the feminist literary journal *Aurora,* and her poetic efforts serve to solidify her fundamental political goal. Her varied poetry, which ranges in subject from love to politics to women, underscores the need for transformation. It is not possible to engage all of her literary or political contributions here (others such as Emilio Zamora and Inés Hernández have already begun to do so); let it suffice to note her passionate argument for the urgent need to create a new female voice, which she presents in her well-known poem "Surge" (Ramírez, in Magón 1980, p. 168):

> Los dioses son arrojados de los templos; los reyes son
>   echados de sus tronos, la mujer es siempre la mujer.

> Los dioses viven lo que sus creyentes quieren. Los reyes
>   viven mientras no son destronados; la mujer vive
>   siempre y este es el secreto de su dicha, vivir.

Sólo la acción es vida; sentir que se vive, es la más hermosa
    sensación.

Surge, pues, a las bellezas de la vida; pero surge así, bella
    de cualidades, esplendente de virtudes, fuerte de
    energías.

Gods are thrown out of temples; kings are driven from
    their thrones, woman is always woman.

Gods live what their followers want. Kings live as long as
    they are not dethroned; woman always lives and this is
    the secret, to live.

Only action is life; to feel that one lives is the most
    beautiful sensation.

Rise up, then, to the beauties of life; but rise up so,
    beautiful with qualities, splendid with virtues, strong
    with energies.

Ramírez envisions change through women's transformation of self and
voice. She, as a magonista, understood that this voice comes out of, is
defined by, and defines the historical moment. Her call in "Surge" goes
out to women as well as to men. She challenges the political struggle to
recreate more humane relationships with society. Her challenge falls, in
this "signifying moment," within women's time and is clearly declared
through women's voice.

As noted earlier, Kristeva refers to that moment of mental signifying
intensity in which the definition of the subject is iterated. We can come to
understand this moment of transformation more clearly through Bakhtin's
notion of the chronotope, which is, literally, time space: "the intrinsic connectedness of temporal and spatial relationships that are artistically expressed in literature. . . . What counts for us is the fact that it expresses the
inseparability of space and time (time as the fourth dimension of space)"
(Bakhtin 1981, p. 84). The intersection of time and history is at the center
of the chronotope. Bakhtin (1981, p. 84) elaborates on this element:

> In the literary artistic chronotope, spatial and temporal in-
> dicators are fused into one carefully thought-out, concrete
> whole. Time, as it were, thickens, takes on flesh, becomes
> artistically visible; likewise, space becomes charged and re-
> sponsive to the movements of time, plot and history. The

intersection of axes and fusion of indicators characterizes the artistic chronotope.

Sara Estela Ramírez's political/literary activity can be said to constitute a type of chronotope in which women's time "takes on flesh, becomes artistically visible," and this moment of signifying intensity becomes a precursor to some contemporary Chicana literary production. For purposes of this discussion, I will briefly examine contemporary writers who through their political and literary activity also iterate the subject through a fusion of time, plot, and history.

Like Ramírez, Cherríe Moraga is poet, essayist, and activist. In the introduction to the first edition of *This Bridge Called My Back: Writings by Radical Women of Color* (1981, p. xiv), she chronicles the excruciating battle that she and Gloria Anzaldúa waged to publish the collection, which she perceived to be an unleashing of women's voices which had been imprisoned through racism, sexism, and indifference: "What drew me to politics was my love of women, the agony I felt in observing the straight-jackets of poverty and repression I saw people in my own family in. But the deepest political tragedy I have experienced is how with such grace, such blind faith, this commitment to women in the feminist movement grew to be exclusive and reactionary. *I call my white sisters on this.*" Moraga views this book as a vehicle for transformation: "I am talking about believing that we have the power to actually transform our experience, change our lives, save our lives. Otherwise, why this book? It is the faith of activists I am talking about" (Moraga and Anzaldúa 1981, p. xviii).

Moraga's borderland is conceived as a gendered space of divisions. In *Bridge*, she presents a manifesto about women's sexual and political relations. Akin to the PLM strategies for Mexican liberation, Moraga's manifesto is also based on the force of women's voice and the articulation of women's time. The oppression she counters is far-reaching and includes the economic poverty that afflicts so many women of color as well as the indifference that some white feminists exhibit toward their voice. Moraga affirms that "even the word 'oppression' has lost its power. We need a new language, better words that can more closely describe women's fear of and resistance to one another; words that will not always come out sounding like dogma" (Moraga and Anzaldúa 1981, p. 30).

Like Sara Estela Ramírez in "Surge," Moraga calls on women to transform themselves, their voice, their historical time. This is the moment of signification, the space in which change is envisioned, in which it "takes on flesh." Moraga calls women to action:

But one voice is not enough, nor two, although this is where dialogue begins. It is essential that radical feminists confront their fear of and resistance to each other, because without this, there *will* be no bread on the table. Simply, we will not survive. If we could make this connection in our heart of hearts, that if we are serious about a revolu-tion—better—if we seriously believe that there should be joy in our lives (real joy, not just "good times"), then we need one another. We women need each other. Because my/your solitary, self-asserting "go-for-the-throat-of-fear" power is not enough. The real power, as you and I well know, is collective. I can't afford to be afraid of you, nor you of me. If it takes head-on collisions, let's do it: this polite timidity is killing us.

. . . it is in looking to the nightmare that the dream is found. There, the survivor emerges to insist on a future, a vision, yes, born out of what is dark and female. The fem-inist movement must be a movement of such survivors, a movement with a future. (p. 34)

Clearly, Moraga recognizes the intensity of this "signifying moment," which spurs on her sense of urgency. Both Ramírez and Moraga form a continuum of "signifying moments" in which the female subject is iter-ated and contested. Their fusion of time, plot, and history, which attends the intensity of their moments, forms a chronotope of transformation for the evolving generations of women's time. As such, this chronotope forms, to use another of Bakhtin's terms, a centrifugal force that counters the cen-tripetal force of authoritative discourse because it disperses the hierarchi-cal stronghold of patriarchy.

La herida abierta:
BORDER AESTHETICS

These voices, speaking at separate ends of the twentieth century, chart the political and creative possibilities of the "emotional residue of an unnatural boundary," returning to Anzaldúa's words, that emanate from the borderlands. They lie on a continuum tied not to place but to symbolic space rooted in political relations.

For Anzaldúa, being a "border woman" places her in an uncomfortable territory: home. This space is geographical, political, racial, and gendered. It is also body and consciousness; it is political. Hence, the body as border becomes the site of consciousness and politics. In the opening poem to her volume *Borderlands/La Frontera*, she brings all these elements together:

> 1,950 mile-long open wound
>> dividing a *pueblo*, a culture,
>> running down the length of my body,
>>> staking fence rods in my flesh,
>>> splits me   splits me
>>>> *me raja   me raja*
>
> This is my home
> this thin edge of
> barbwire

This home does not accept her either as a Mexicana—a woman—or as a lesbian. Her discomfort stems from the political legacy of the territory and her gendered status: "Alienated from her mother culture, 'Alien' in the dominant culture, the woman of color does not feel safe within the inner life of her self. Petrified, she can't respond, her face caught between los intersticios, the space between the different worlds she inhabits" (p. 20). Anzaldúa does not negate the obscurity of that outsiderhood; she claims it: "I am a turtle, wherever I go I carry 'home' on my back" (p. 21). Her body becomes the site for inscribing the ambiguity of her history and existence. It is the site for her creative energies, the locus of her discourse, which emerges directly from a reconstruction of Aztec and Chicana histories. By recovering the feminine potential in Coatlicue, she rewrites the history of Chicanos, which was written during the Movement (mostly by males), and affirms the multiplicities represented by the serpent goddess. Through Coatlicue, Anzaldúa derives a creative center that directs her as a mestiza and as a creative artist:

> During the dark side of the moon something in the mirror
> catches my gaze, I seem all eyes and nose. Inside my skull
> something shifts. I "see" my face. Gloria, the everyday
> face; Prieta and Prietita, my childhood faces; Gaudi, the
> face my mother and sister and brothers know. And there
> in the black, obsidian mirror of the Nahuas is yet another
> face, a stranger's face. Simultáneamente me miraba la cara
> desde distintos ángulos. Y mi cara, como la realidad, tenía
> un caracter multiplice. (Simultaneously I saw my face
> from different angles. And my face, like reality, had a
> multiple character.) (p. 44; my translation)

Anzaldúa recognizes that, like Coatlicue, she reflects not duality but rather a third perspective—something more than a synthesis of duality—she is contradictory and achieves her character from an incarnation of multiplicity. She links this process directly to the body:

> When I write it feels like I'm carving bone. It feels like I'm creating my own face, my own heart—a Nahuatl concept. My soul makes itself through the creative act. It is constantly remaking and giving birth to itself through my body. . . .
>
> For only through the body, through the pulling of flesh, can the human soul be transformed. And for images, words, stories to have this transformative power, they must arise from the human body—flesh and bone—and from the earth's body—stone, sky, liquid, soil. (pp. 73–75)

Anzaldúa merges geopolitics with spirituality/creativity; that is, she reconstructs a personal/political history in order to articulate the "New Mestiza Consciousness," which is physically inscribed and which is central to her vision of transformation: "And once again I recognize that the internal tension of oppositions can propel (if it doesn't tear apart) the mestiza writer out of the *metate* where she is being ground with corn and water, eject her out as a *nahual*, an agent of transformation, able to modify and shape primordial energy and therefore able to change herself and others into turkey, coyote, tree, or human" (p. 74).

This power of transformation is located in the mouth of the serpent goddess Coatlicue, a space guarded by rows of fierce teeth, the site of entrance and of grinding together, the source of power and of language. The mestiza writer, by constructing her own discourse of contradiction, ambiguity, and multiplicity, voices her creative/political self through a fusion of body, sex, and symbol.

In her autobiography, *Loving in the War Years: Lo que nunca pasó por sus labios,* Cherríe Moraga explores the political through the personal. The borderland that emerges complicates the continuum. Her poem "Raw Experience" presents a meditation about race and gender conceived of as a search for connections, which she symbolizes by the use of three bridges into herself.

In the first movement of this poem, Moraga is split off from herself; she is watching herself for clues to who she is and where she might be going. Her visage is in constant movement, as her face becomes "a moving portrait / in a storefront window," and she is taken aback by seeing her own face, "sinking into itself." But a motor inside herself propels her forward, even as she looks outwardly for evidence of her being: "I watch myself for clues, / trying to catch up / inhabit my body / again" (Moraga 1983, p. 49). The claiming of the self is a process involving an active assertion of being in the face of nonbeing or indeterminate space. For this reason, the second movement of the poem begins by asserting a symbolic space in which she can locate and inscribe this in-between motion of being. The view of three bridges gives her options for identification: "a color / an island / a view of the red rock." Each of these possibilities projects an undesignated destination: "Each with a particular destination / coming and going." She invests in these spaces the probability of her life, because at this point she inverses the phrase she has reiterated throughout the poem and says instead: "I watch *them* [my emphasis] for clues." There she will find the life force of her being: "their secrets / about making connections / about getting / someplace."

The connections are invested in the bridges themselves, which in their being connote probability of relating, of arriving at some understanding. It is important to note that Moraga does not get to the other side of the bridge, so to speak; rather, she takes comfort in the indeterminacy itself. The process of finding "clues," finding connections, is affirmed in this liminal space of Moraga's creative consciousness.

I have deliberately chosen to discuss a poem that does not deal with the border (that is, the physical space between Mexico and the United States) per se in order to underscore a larger point. The border has come to be for many Chicana writers an aspect of their critical subjectivity in which they position themselves, usually with images of bridges or other locators of liminal space. This space is a creative moment of gender/political symbolic designation in which the writer inscribes self and affirms her connections with women of different races or nationalities who experience the same creative force of their constantly defining selves.

Cherríe Moraga is notable, among other things, for her creative efforts with other radical women of color. Her noted anthology *This Bridge Called My Back*, co-edited with Gloria Anzaldúa, graphically portrays the literary/political bridges connecting women of varied races. In *Loving in the War Years*, Moraga looks to herself in order to discover the connections in her personal experience that will lead her to form political ties with other Chicanas. Her essay "A Long Line of Vendidas" is a polemical assertion of meaning and connection. At the end of that work, she again turns into herself in order to locate the space that will signify her power to transform herself and fuel her creative being:

En el sueño mi amor me pregunta "Donde está tu río?"
And I point to the middle of my chest.

   I am a river cracking open. It's as if the parts of me
were just thin tributaries. Lines of water like veins running
barely beneath the soil or skimming the bone surface of
the earth—sometimes desert creek, sometimes city-wash,
sometimes like sweat sliding down a woman's breastbone.

   Now I can see the point of juncture. Comunión. And I
gather my forces to make the river run. (p. 145)

The river of creation, of life (the quintessential "Río Grande," if you
will), that points to a juncture or division is contained within herself and
in her articulation of racial and gendered locations of self: "desert creek,"
"city-wash," "a woman's breastbone." Only in this symbolic space can the
poet make communion and sanctify the process of her creative being:
"And I gather my forces to make the river run." She claims herself to be
the creator of her own life force.

   Pat Mora claims her space by affirming connections to seemingly traditional symbolic spaces. As Rebolledo points out, "the natural landscape
becomes personified, and she transforms the desert into the mother/
teacher and the narrator into the mediator." Undoubtedly, the desert informs Mora's sense of self. She comes from a tradition of women writers
who see the physical landscape as a creative vortex of their art. In fact, in a
poem dedicated to Georgia O'Keeffe, Mora articulates her relationship to
this tradition: "I want / to walk / with you / on my Texas desert, . . . to
see your fingers / pick a bone bouquet / touching life / where I touch
death, . . . / to feel you touch / my eyes / as you touch canvas / to unfold /
giant blooms" (Mora 1984, p. 43). The "giant blooms" of Mora's poems
continue the sensual tradition of O'Keeffe's passion for the Southwest.
Rebolledo has already analyzed Mora's use of the Texas desert as an in-
forming female principle in her writing. Here I would like to carry this
analysis further by exploring the expansive symbolic designation of space
that Mora extrapolates in her poems. The Texas desert and the El Paso
border become symbolic designators of her stance as a Chicana and as
a poet.

   Like Ramírez, Anzaldúa, and Moraga, Mora is a poet, essayist, and activist.[2] She explores the indeterminate space of her symbolic creation,
which becomes a primary locator for herself as an ethnic, gendered, and
class-informed person. In this intermediate space, the contradictions that
constitute her political and poetic self are exposed. In Anzaldúa's terms, in

this borderland Mora dramatizes the *herida abierta* in which worlds grate against each other and bleed.

In the poem "Illegal Alien" the poet sits in her "yellow kitchen" while the woman servant who has been hired from across the border talks about physical abuse by her husband. The woman devastatingly announces to the middle-class woman poet: "We don't fight with words on that side of the Río Grande." Neither do they sympathize with women who have the luxury of writing poems, while they work. The poet understands the class contradiction that is so graphically revealed and she can only offer a futile conditional: "I offer foolish questions / when I should hug you hard, / when I should dry your eyes, my sister, / sister because we are both women, / both married, both warmed / by Mexican blood" (1984, p. 40). But the conditional is not enough, and the inadequacy of the poet to change the conditions of exploitation is brought home: "It is not cool words you need / but soothing hands. / My plastic band-aid doesn't fit / your hurt. / I am the alien here" (p. 40). The speaker understands that she comes out of a "plastic" ersatz world whose remedies are ineffectual. She does not even have the words, which for a poet is no small statement, to alleviate the pain of her sister. But the sisterhood is divided by class, by a border that exists in real terms for the speaker in this poem for the first time.

Yet this middle space of divisions in which we attempt to find meaning can also affirm connections. In "Sonrisas," the speaker's in-between placement allows her to penetrate two worlds and to juxtapose their affective states of being:

> I live in a doorway
> between two rooms. I hear
> quiet clicks, cups of black
> coffee, *click, click* like facts
>   budgets, tenure, curriculum,
> from careful women in crisp beige
> suits, quick beige smiles
> that seldom sneak into their eyes.
>
> I peek
> in the other room señoras
> in faded dresses stir sweet
> milk coffee, laughter whirls
> with steam from fresh *tamales*
> *sh, sh, mucho ruido,*

they scold one another,
press their lips, trap smiles
in their dark, Mexican eyes. (p. 20)

The speaker contrasts the "click, click" of the fact-oriented world of the university with the "sh, sh" of the coffee room of the workers. The black coffee is juxtaposed to the sweet swirls of *café con leche*. The opposition of the worlds is an ordinary one. It is couched within the common parlance of stereotype: the cold, isolated Anglo world versus the warm, communal world of the Mexican. But the substance of the poem does not rest in turning a stereotypic phrase; rather it resides in the stance of the poet who does not locate herself in either world. As we recall, she does not say that she is "standing" in the doorway between two rooms; no, she "lives" in this doorway opening up two worldviews that she can penetrate through her poetic perception, which, she understands, is perception only. The poet does not reside, belong, or claim either determined space—a space that has been determined by others. Her suspension has yet to be transformed into a creative space of self designation.

In the poem ending her first book of poetry, *Chants*, Mora laments her hyphenated self as the token cultural hybrid. The title of the poem attests to the legitimization of her intermediate status: "Legal Alien." In this poem, being bilingual and bicultural is a way to be twice disaffected: "American but hyphenated, / viewed by Anglos as perhaps exotic, / perhaps inferior, definitely different, / viewed by Mexicans as alien, . . . an American to Mexicans / A Mexican to Americans." Not claimed by either world, the poet understands the liminality of her position: "a handy token / sliding back and forth / between the fringes of both worlds" (p. 52). This uncomfortable state underscores the rigid racial/ethnic divisions that exacerbate this poet's status within her borderline world. Indeed, these two poems ("Sonrisas" and "Legal Alien") vividly create the image of Anzaldúa's borderland: "a vague and undetermined place created by the emotional residue of an unnatural boundary," a place, she adds, that is in "a constant state of transition." It is to this aspect of the border, particularly with respect to gender, that Mora's second book of poems, *Borders*, addresses itself more clearly.[3]

The title poem of the volume opens with a quote from Carol Gilligan: "My research suggests that men and women may speak different languages that they assume are the same." Mora rejoins with a question: "If we're so bright / why didn't we notice?" The notion of language, or more accurately discourses, as a barrier to communication is explored in the three movements of this poem, which act as prologue to her collection.

I
The side-by-side translations
were the easy ones.
Our tongues tasted *luna*
chanting, chanting to the words
it touched; our lips circled
moon sighing its longing.
We knew: similar but different.

II
And we knew of grown-up talk,
how even in our own home
like became unlike,
how the child's singsong

                                               I want, I want

burned our mouth
when we whispered in the dark.

III
But us? You and I
who've talked for years
tossing words back and forth

                                            success, happiness

back and forth
over coffee, over wine
at parties, in bed
and I was sure you heard,
        u n d e r s t o o d,
though now I think of it
I can remember screaming
to be sure.

So who can hear
the words we speak
you and I, like but unlike,
and translate us to us
side by side?

(1986, PP. 9–10)

    The first movement posits language, that is English/Spanish, as an analog to other problematic discourses—gender, ethnicity (or culture), and class. The assertion that an easy side-by-side translation can be achieved is belied by the speaker's complex statement of equivalency, made in the first stanza. The "tongues" do not utter the word "moon" in Spanish, *luna*, they *taste* its sensual attributes, making an incantation to objects or "words" touched by the experience of *luna*. The moon is a perennial metaphor for femininity, and here the gender connotation is being manipulated, as is the cultural locator contained in the Spanish word. The concomitant statement about *moon* is also tied to an activity of claiming the object as "our lips circled / *moon* sighing its longing." The tasting and circling of the mouth around the moon represents the ingestion of female gender. It is an active claiming of the cultural, gendered self that is expanded by the English "translation." For this reason, the speaker understands the interdependence of the worldviews presented by each discourse (*luna*, moon): "We knew: similar but different."

Essential to understanding the oppositions in the poem is noting the use of the pronouns (our, we), which places the equivalency statement within one community. No Anglo versus Mexican contrast is being made here. Those cultural and gender divisions have been internalized in the speaker. The "we" to whom she refers includes women, Mexicans, and others to whom "similar but different" is a statement of their liminal status.

The second movement uses the discourse of human development to explore another set of divisions. Here the children must make sense of "grown-up talk." Through this talk they have been taught about the perceptions of different peoples and been instructed in economic and class bias. They learn that "Like became unlike," and the seeds of material longing ("I want, I want") are burned into their mouths and into their psyches. The "singsong" is ingrained early, this discourse of class, material success, and discontent.

In the third movement, the speaker changes to a personal direct address. The question now is how to unravel the distinctions that have divided and prevented communication. The addressee of the poem has, for many years, been engaged with the speaker in a sustained dialogue about contested issues: "*success, happiness,*" two words connoting various interpretations of value. But the dialogue disintegrates into silences as the speaker recalls "screaming / to be sure" that her partner has understood. But as the hearing abled usually deal with the hearing impaired, she screams—as if volume will supersede the fundamental silence between them. The final stanza is an appeal for intervention, for someone who will "hear / the words we speak" and who will translate their languages into a bridge of communication. The poet does not overcome the discourses bordering her in and keeping her out of different spheres, she only asks the question that the rest of her poems in the collection will attempt to address.

This poem presents us with a symbolic space of multiple borders that divide on the bases of gender, ethnicity, and class. The poet positions herself in an indeterminate space, which in itself has value, for it places into question all those "languages" or perceptions that isolate us into our silent and, at times, hostile worlds.

Mora counters this meditation on the ever-widening borderlands of our own making with poems that claim a voice and a symbolic space, poems that carry within them the power of the primal forces of the earth. In "Desert Women" (1986, p. 80), Mora likens women to the cactus plant, a figure of survival: "Like cactus / we've learned to hoard, / to sprout deep roots, / to seem asleep, yet wake / at the scent of softness / in the air, to hide / pain and loss by silence, / no branches wail / or whisper our sad songs / safe behind our thorns." But the force of creativity is there under the hard skin and thorns: "Don't be deceived. / When we bloom, we stun." The inside/outside, silence/scream binaries that form Mora's particular border gestalt are superseded in discrete moments of claiming meaning and self, for the cactus not only flowers, it stuns—that is, it controls through its brilliance.

Art is a forceful vector in claiming power from the indeterminate space of the border. The southwestern desert is a physical, cultural, and political border born out of the cultural and political conflicts of conquest, but it is also, as I have shown, a larger symbolic designation in which the nexus of race, class, and gender become actively articulated. These writers are engaged in a cultural critique that alters our discourses about ourselves and alters the historical moment. Adrienne Rich (1979, p. 35) has noted that "a radical critique of literature, feminist in its impulse, would take the work first of all as a clue to how we live, how we have been living, how we have been led to imagine ourselves, how our language has trapped as well as liberated us, how the very act of naming has been till now a male prerogative, and how we can begin to see and name—and therefore live—afresh."

Because women's time and voice have unfolded, the border is no longer dominated by male-centered cultural nationalist definitions of conflict. Chicana writers claim this space as a significant symbolic denominator for their expansive understanding of exploitation and survival. As Anzaldúa concludes, "to survive the Borderlands / you must live *sin fronteras* / be a crossroads." Within the gaze of these writers, the border is reformed and renamed as woman, not as a lady with pretensions of class, nor a man with pretensions of superiority, but as a person who glories in the sensuality of the life she draws from the arid sand. In "unrefined" by Pat Mora the desert is symbolically designated as a woman who dances and screams and, like a whirlwind, gathers within her motion all that surrounds her:

> The desert is no lady.
> She screams at the spring sky,
> dances with her skirts high,
> kicks sand, flings tumbleweeds,
> digs her nails into all flesh,
> Her unveiled lust fascinates the sun (1984, p. 8)

It is a fitting poem with which to close this discussion, because it affirms that the symbolic space of "the doorway between two rooms" is also the location of power, a power transformed by the female gaze into a process of continual possibility.

When someone with the authority of a teacher, say,
describes the world and you are not in it, there is this
moment of psychic disequilibrium, as if you looked
into a mirror and saw nothing.

ADRIENNE RICH
"Invisibility in Academe,"
in *Blood, Bread, and Poetry: Selected Prose 1979–1985*

You must understand that in the attempt to correct so
many generations of bad faith and cruelty, when it is
operating not only in the classroom but in society,
you will meet the most fantastic, the most brutal,
and the most determined resistance. There is
no point in pretending that this won't happen.

JAMES BALDWIN
"A Talk to Teachers"

From this racial, ideological, cultural and biological
cross-pollinization, an "alien" consciousness is
presently in the making—a new *mestiza* consciousness,
una conciencia de mujer. It is a consciousness of the
Borderlands.

GLORIA ANZALDÚA
Borderlands/La Frontera

Borderness
and Pedagogy

EXPOSING CULTURE

IN THE CLASSROOM

Acknowledgment of the cultural annihilation to which Adrienne Rich alerts us in the first epigraph to this chapter has begun to alter what we teach and how we teach it. Because of this new awareness, the classroom has become the focal point of theoretical and practical debate regarding the viability of certain culturally diverse materials for instruction and the effects of this material on the values and the future of life as they have been known in the United States. For those of us who have attempted to realize change in the institutionalized center of cultural formation and dissemination—the classroom—the debate has led to vociferous and at times discomfiting opposition.

Turning the collective gaze of the classroom to an examination of culture, which includes consideration of the effects of difference (gender, race, class, and ethnicity), is not a comfortable or a highly prized objective of most institutions of education. The rhetoric of diversity, such as celebration of our culture as the great melting pot or the freshest salad bowl, belies the ambivalence and fear of difference so pervasive in our society. This fear finds its greatest rootedness in differences of race and gender.

The issue is not just an insider/outsider problem, a simple we/they opposition, or a masculine/feminine construction. Nor is the issue just a matter of access to a dominant culture. Rather, it is a questioning of culture as determined by conscious and unconscious policies of exclusion based on inequalities perceived in some cultural differences. Many scholars, critics, artists, and political activists have complicated the debate by realigning the issues along progressive lines—that is, through consideration of the perspectives of people of color.

Color, however, is not necessarily equivalent to our inherited notions of race or ethnicity. Even now, when speaking of race, most people refer to a black/white racial binary. Yet the notion of race, as we all know, is far more problematic. The "Other" that is stigmatized by race is not confined to

African Americans, Asian Americans, or Native Americans. Some ethnic "Others" are perceived as racial, particularly in certain incarnations of oppositional culture; moreover, some manifestations of gender differences are similarly stigmatized. What we have here is an intersection of race, ethnicity, and gender, which the self-designation "people of color" underscores by making the larger, stigmatized "Other" visible and a vortex of political solidarity.

The perspective of "people of color" indicates an acceptance of racialness not only as inevitable, but as a creative focal point for art, politics, and education. The performance artist Guillermo Gómez-Peña, who finds himself between nations, languages, and monetary and artistic economies, claims himself as one of the "children of the chasm that is opening between the 'first' and the 'third' worlds." He too is one of the indisputable heirs to a new *mestizaje* (the fusion of the Amerindian and European races)" (1988, p. 130). He concludes: "As a result of this process I have become a cultural topographer, border-crosser, and hunter of myths. And it doesn't matter where I find myself, in Califas or Mexico City, or Barcelona or West Berlin; I always have the sensation that I belong to the same species: the migrant tribe of fiery pupils" (p. 128).

We are all implicated in this chasm "between the 'first' and the 'third' worlds," because those "fiery pupils" find themselves in our classrooms; the literature we are attempting to integrate into the curriculum emerges from this zone. Is acknowledging this situation of "Otherness" and incorporating culturally diverse texts into the curriculum enough? Indeed it is not. We can no longer assume that a common culture exists into which these "recalcitrant cultural anomalies" can be made to fit. The dream of a common culture is gone, and we have in its place a dynamic flowering of multiplicities. The crisis of identity does not lie within the cultural "Other" but within United States society itself. Gómez-Peña (1988, p. 129) gives us an insight into this situation:

> I am a child of crisis and cultural syncretism, half hippie
> and half punk. My generation grew up watching movies
> about cowboys and science fiction, listening to *cumbias* and
> tunes from the Moody Blues, constructing altars and film-
> ing in Super-8, reading the *Corno Emplumado* and *Artforum*,
> traveling to Tepoztlán and San Francisco, creating and de-
> creating myths. We went to Cuba in search of political il-
> lumination, to Spain to visit the crazy grandmother and
> to the U.S. in search of the instantaneous musico-sexual

paradise. We found nothing. Our dreams wound up getting caught in the webs of the border.

Gómez-Peña and his generation are not the only ones caught within
that web. This syncretism of cultures aptly describes the cultural situation
of the United States itself. And borderness, a consciousness of living in
the borderlands, is a useful empathetic tool for understanding the discomfort that educators who face the "web of the border" feel when we enter
classrooms throughout this country.

Henry Louis Gates, in different terms, articulates a similar political understanding when he writes in his introduction to his collection of essays
Loose Canons: Notes on the Culture Wars (1992, p. xv):

> Ours is a late-twentieth-century world profoundly fissured
> by nationality, ethnicity, race, class, and gender. And the
> only way to transcend those divisions—to forge, for once,
> a civic culture that respects both differences and common-
> alities—is through education that seeks to comprehend
> the diversity of human culture. Beyond the hype and the
> high-flown rhetoric is a pretty homely truth: There is no
> tolerance without respect—and no respect without
> knowledge.

Similarly, in an address at the University of California, Riverside (1991),
Cornel West remarks that "we as human beings are part of civilizations
that have always had ambiguous legacies, cultures that are always already
hybrid that are built on the elements and fragments of antecedent cultures.
So that the notion of pristine cultures falls by the wayside." Consequently,
for West, a critical sensibility that recovers an understanding of difference
as integral to cultural production is one that is rooted in a moral imperative. He explains that "it is a perspective that forces us to understand any
society, any culture in terms of its complexity, how in fact we as human
beings interact with one another" (unpublished oral recording).

Yet Guillermo Gómez-Peña's staggering demographics quoted in Chapter 5 further complicate the dimensions of this morality play. His multi-
racial, multigendered border culture alters the mix in the proverbial pot.
As it is, the ideology of "Americanness" in terms of race has been characterized by a simple binary, whether that be "us versus them" or "black versus white" rhetoric. Gómez-Peña's incipient manifesto shatters once again
the dream of a common culture that is based on the illusion of civility and
civic participation. The interaction among peoples in the United States

traditionally has not been characterized by equality or common sharing of power and social control. It has been marked by a need to normalize, to reduce cultural hybridity into its lowest common denominator in order, many have believed, to effect a manageable idea of cultural and national identity. But that common culture—as West, Gómez-Peña, and Gates among others have pointed out—has been based on obfuscation, cultural destruction, and repression of difference. The ideal of a common culture did not reflect the reality of the increasingly hybrid cultural profile that has been shown to be historically resilient and permanent.

Many have feared that difference only divides; it cannot bind peoples together under one national rubric. Yet if we understand difference as the common cultural reference point it becomes the basis for unity—a paradoxical concept that has proven difficult for many to grasp. At the root of this paradox is an imperative that releases us from the debilitating tension between anarchy and order that has characterized the ways in which culture, invariably conceived as icon, has driven our social order including our educational system. The "rage for order" dominates Allan Bloom and E. D. Hirsch's manifestos as well as Arthur Schlesinger's more recent concern about the "fraying of American Culture." Their ideas fundamentally reflect a fear of anarchy. Yet a critical sensibility that deals with cultural hybridity as a resource puts into play other terms of analysis that point to the enabling complexities of our cultural multiplicities and reestablishes a self-critical moment in which we regain the richness and cultural resources that have been denied through the urge to reduce, to make common. This is a moment in which we redirect our agenda as educators and as participants in civic culture.

So if—and this is a big if—the question about "What is to be done?" has been addressed, the follow-up question "How do we do it?" has not. Do we argue for a form of common culture through "exposure" to other cultures through texts? Does this agenda mask a call for a form of that consensus out of which the "Americanization" programs of the turn of the century proceeded?

In a critique of the theoretical positing of the consensus versus descent paradigm advocated by Werner Sollors, Ramón Saldívar (1991, p. 19) cautions:

> The American ideological consensus . . . takes on a very different quality when we take into account the ways that class origins and racial and gender differences affect literary and social history. At the very least, people of different

classes, races, and gender will feel the effects of that consensus and its hegemony differently. And if Jameson's notion of expressive causality is to be taken seriously as a
way of regarding history as the "absent cause" accessible
to us only through its "narrativization in the political unconscious," then we must not easily dismiss the real power
of difference to resist the reifying tendencies of studies
such as Sollors' with their presumptuous claims to move
"beyond ethnicity" toward the formation of an unitary
American culture.

What do a theory of difference and a pedagogy of difference have in
common? How does the experience of difference translate into the classroom environment? The answer necessitates sustaining a delicate balance
between theory and practice. At the same time that critics have argued for
an unmasking of the political suppositions undergirding the traditional
canon, they have also at times consciously and unconsciously supported
the goal of the classroom as the site of political transformation. Henry
Louis Gates (*Loose Canons*, pp. xiii–xiv) correctly observes:

> But is the political and social significance of our work as
> immediate as all that? Or is the noisy spectacle of the pub-
> lic debate a kind of stage behind which far narrower gains
> are secured or relinquished? I must confess to considerable
> ambivalence on the matter. The "larger issues" that frame
> the classroom clamor are profoundly real: but the signifi-
> cance of our own interventions is easily over-stated; and
> I do not exempt myself from this admonition.

Either the political nature of pedagogy is perceived to be tantamount to
a national betrayal or the classroom is indeed a limited space of transformation. The answer lies, again, somewhere in between, in the teacher's imperative to "teach," to establish new frameworks for interacting together.
In *Race Matters* (1993, p. 4), Cornel West argues for the necessity for a moral
understanding of the American "Educational" project:

> To establish a new framework, we need to begin with a
> frank acknowledgment of the basic humanness and Ameri-
> canness of each of us. And we must acknowledge that as a
> people—*E Pluribus Unum*—we are on a slippery slope to-
> ward economic strife, social turmoil, and cultural chaos.
> If we go down, we go down together. The Los Angeles

upheaval forced us to see not only that we are not connected in ways we would like to be but also, in a more
profound sense, that this failure to connect binds us even
more tightly together. The paradox of race in America is
that our common destiny is more pronounced and imper-
iled precisely when our divisions are deeper.

Those divisions are multiple. They are race, class, gender, sexuality,
and linguistically based. And it is in the classroom that these divisions are
played out most dynamically. The refractions of difference are stagger-
ingly multiple, as Gloria Anzaldúa (1987, pp. 77–78) eloquently reminds us:

> Because I, a *mestiza*,
> continually walk out of one culture
> and into another,
> because I am in all cultures at the same time,
> *alma de dos mundos, tres, cuatro,*
> *me zumba la cabeza con lo contradictorio.*
> *Estoy norteada por todas las voces que me hablan*
> *simultáneamente.*

In a constant state of mental nepantilism, an Aztec
word meaning torn between ways, *la mestiza* is a product
of the transfer of the cultural and spiritual values of one
group to another. Being tricultural, monolingual, bilingual,
or multilingual, speaking in a patois, and in a state of perpetual transition, the *mestiza* faces the dilemma of the
mixed breed: which collectivity does the daughter of a
darkskinned mother listen to?

The dilemma of the mestiza resonates in the dilemma of the Americas,
and in particular the United States. It is a dilemma that in many ways informs the pedagogical situation when we as professors and as students are
called upon to educate and to be educated in the paradigmatic border
space of the classroom. In Anzaldúa's theorizing about *mestizaje*, the only
way to survive the borderlands is to acknowledge the multiplicity of difference and to acquire a tolerance for ambiguity. I suggest that herein lies that
edge on which we might leverage both a theory and practice of difference.

With her book *Borderlands / La Frontera* Gloria Anzaldúa has emerged as
a major theorist regarding borderness and border consciousness, ideas
that have become useful particularly for critics of Chicano/a and Latino/a
literatures. In this volume she posits a problematic of contradiction. As

explained above, she asks the hard questions about the effects of cultural multiplicity: "which collectivity does the daughter of a darkskinned mother listen to?" And she claims, as we all would like to, that the "answer to the problem between the white race and the colored, between males and females, lies in healing the split that originates in the very foundation of our lives, our cultures, our languages, our thoughts" (p. 78). The consciousness of the mestiza is the key to that healing. It is a coming together based on race, ethnicity, class, and gender. It is a vortex of difference. Anzaldúa concludes that we must all empathetically project ourselves into the borderland and from there change the "symbolic contract" with which we have been defined: "To survive the Borderlands / you must live *sin fronteras* / be a crossroads (p. 195).

Being a crossroads does not imply a denial of difference; rather it promotes an articulation of difference. It means living without borders, but it also means living as an intersection of all the border spaces that define: race, class, gender, sexuality, ethnicity. Norma Alarcón has argued, along with other feminists of color, that there can be no totalizing "we" female subject. Similarly there can be no essential "we" of a "common culture." Chicana feminists are calling into question the imperative to homogenize, particularly in mainstream feminist theory. Seeking ways to uncover multiplicity in theory is an equally challenging prospect in the classroom. The complexity of this theoretical and pedagogical project clearly underscores that merely changing the course lists is not enough.

Race, gender, and sexuality among other elements inform border consciousness and contribute to the problematic nature of a pedagogical project that attempts to expose the multiplicity of cultures. As mentioned above, to be conscious of the borderlands is to tolerate ambiguity since the search for homogeneity is frustrated in the border regions. Thus to change the lists is not sufficient. If the subjectivities of teacher and student are not questioned, exposed, integrated into the process of the classroom, then the "reading" or even "rereading" of texts will not make a qualitative difference. We must ask ourselves as feminists and as educators, "What is our objective in the classroom?" Is it to "expose" students to a new angle on Western culture or is it to transform their and our relationship to culture?

Central to understanding this point is acknowledging that the classroom is a politicized space. It has always been a politicized space because the systems of thought, as well as cultural and political hierarchies, are affirmed and denied there. In the classroom, authority and, as we all know, patriarchy are replicated. Do we carry on the traditions of those systems which we learned in the classrooms of our childhoods, colleges, and graduate schools? Do we avert this by merely reading Chicana, Native American, African American, or Asian American texts? Clearly, integrating these texts into the curriculum is a necessary first step, but it must be followed by redefining the classroom itself as a process externalizing the intersections of race, class, ethnicity, and gender that underlie all texts—as well as the text of the classroom itself.

Adrienne Rich has written about the various manifestations of the "culture of passivity." We internalize and perpetuate old systems by not asking questions, by accepting a situation as if it were the natural order of things. And this applies to the "old" canon, as well as to the reconstruction of the "new" canon. If we do not account for our own subjectivity in the classroom, then we risk what Rich calls "passive collusion" in the process of accepting the world always according to someone else, whether that be Emerson, Thoreau, or Cherríe Moraga. As teachers in a classroom, either we can participate in a passive collusion with the culture of passivity or we can attempt to become agents of transformation and thus begin to forge an active culture that acknowledges the true catalytic power of difference.

The issue should not rest solely within our ability as teachers to effect this active culture. Students must also become agents in this transformation. Ernesto Cardenal, Nicaraguan poet and activist, used "exteriorization" as a core process in his poetry workshops that functioned as the building blocks of literacy in his country. The objective was not to interpret, not to embellish, but to make concrete the individual's experience; and words are the concrete vehicles for translating subjectivity to exteriorization. As N. Scott Momaday explains in *The Names* (1976), "had I known it, even then language bore all the names of my being." We need not replicate the model of the poetry workshop, but we do need to underscore the notion that the classroom, workshop if you will, can be a creative space in which students and teachers alike work through their subjectivity to achieve an externalization of the intersecting elements of race, class, ethnicity, and gender that define us all. In other words, the political nature of the classroom can be externalized in a process in which the nexus of race, class, and gender is questioned and activated. In this situation, the student is not just "informed," "taught," or "exposed"; rather, the class together *informs, teaches,* and *exposes.* The focus is on the process, not on the informational product.

This is not an easy task, as we all know. If a form of communitas (to borrow Victor Turner's term) is momentarily achieved within the communal space of the classroom, tensions also threaten to pull it apart. We have all experienced the resistance and denial that accompany the reading of all literature, especially culturally different, linguistically diverse texts. When we are attempting to divest the classroom of its authoritative structure and mode of analysis, who will mediate between clashing subjectivities? The answer is that all persons involved in the learning project will have to do so. As each participant is decentered in the class process, each in some fashion becomes an educator and a student. Each assumes an interactive role with the others. In this sense, we must work through this discomfort with texts and use that resistance to expose difference. Only in this way can we combat the silence that, unfortunately, we have all had to contend with in the traditional classrooms of our past and that falls over into the classrooms of our own making.

Richard Yarborough suggests that we use the notion of diverse "voices" that speak the multiplicity of cultures when we talk about texts. To this fruitful direction, I would add that the voices are not only those of the texts, but also those of the students, teachers, and other participants in the learning project. We cannot understand the difference in voice of a text without understanding our own voice and difference in relationship to it. By focusing on this type of conversation, the classroom can become a space in which a vibrant new discourse can qualitatively challenge the official dominant discourse of the canon. It is a conversation in which questions are asked, contradictions are exposed, and no solutions are reached. In order to teach the new canon, we must be able to live with contradiction, ambiguity, and nonclosure. Although frequently uncomfortable, the process is at the very least consciously active. By participating in this fluid space (the classroom) in which contradictions and conflict are played out, we can create an empathetic moment in which the classroom participants feel what it might be like to cross into the borderlands. Anzaldúa reminds us that the border is a transitional space in which differences are articulated and a "tolerance for ambiguity" is an operational mode. Yet this type of activity will strain everyone's tolerance for ambiguity.

I recently organized a seminar for college seniors called "Chicano Literature in a Cross-Cultural Perspective" that used Chicano literature and its formulation of the border as a paradigm for understanding other culturally diverse writing by African Americans, Asian Americans, Caribbean Islanders, and other Latinos. I began by studying three Chicano texts and analyzing their representation of the border. The final text in this initial unit was *Borderlands/La Frontera* by Anzaldúa, a feminist, lesbian writer, and activist. The students' reactions to the first two texts, which were by male authors, were at times difficult since issues of race and cultural difference were not easy for them to address. The discussions of Chicano history, the reading of the texts, and finally the reference to contemporary issues produced uncomfortable responses, particularly from students of color. Indeed, Adrienne Rich correctly names the detrimental effects of never seeing yourself in the "mirror" of literature as a profound "disequilibrium." At the same time, internalized racial biases surfaced, and reluctant understanding of difference within racial communities was addressed more than prejudice within the dominant culture.

When Anzaldúa's text was read, however, all students (male and female, white/nonwhite) reacted swiftly and severely. Sexuality and issues of sexual orientation clearly elicit fear across the board, regardless of race or class. The discussions were painful and substantive, ranging from a critical assessment of Anzaldúa's aesthetics based on lesbianism to a reluctant review of homophobia within families and university classrooms. Issues such as "outing" and homophobic joking provoked uncomfortable, yet engaged discussion. The debate was heated. At one point, I asked the students to describe the kinds of emotions that had surfaced during the hour of critical dialogue. Once they had analyzed and chronicled their responses and engagement in the discussion, I addressed the main objective of the lesson: the discomfort they felt was analogous to experiencing the border. Their feelings of conflict, discomfort, excitement, moments of confusion and clarification, contradictions and solidarities placed them empathetically in the border zone. They were not expected to resolve either their feelings or the issues; but they had instead exposed their racial, gendered, and class selves in an active performance of difference.

One of the by-products of this class experience was a borrowing and lending across borders that occurred for a transient time. I would not characterize this process as "consciousness-raising" (a form of pedagogy of which, along with Henry Louis Gates, I have a deep suspicion). Consciousness-raising connotes a permanent transformation of consciousness. The illuminations I am seeking are at their best transient. They may appear for a brief time and then retreat. The classroom, like the border, is a transitory space. The transformation of culture is not secured; at best it can be activated. And this occurs through the reading of the texts under assignment and through the self-reflexive "reading" of the text of the class. I don't know whether a form of coalition building based on a knowledge of difference is reached at any given moment. Perhaps. I tend to think of each classroom experience as another layer drawn on the palimpsest of a student's education. With any luck, the residue of that layer will emerge at future times. Perhaps it is key to achieving what Cornel West has called "a prophetic framework of moral reasoning rather than a narrow framework of racial reasoning." Perhaps through a borrowing and lending across borders some sort of articulation of moral and civic culture will emerge that better reflects the enabling resources of our multiple differences. Yet it is not a comfortable place to be. Anzaldúa the poet puts it for us best: "This is my home / this thin edge of / barbwire."

Like Anzaldúa's "edge of barbwire," our society and its future lie in jeopardy in the educational institutions of our nation. In order to survive, our classrooms must "be a crossroads." We must acknowledge that due to our racial, class, and gendered subjectivities we have all been caught in the implications of the "web of the border." It is a place of creative learning; it is the site of our survival. And it is clear that our ability to connect theory and pedagogy is critical to this survival. I hope that the essays in this volume form a small contribution to this project.

Notes

1. "IN OUR OWN LAND"

1. I take Chicano literature to denote literary production by Mexicans or persons of Mexican descent living in the United States. Although other Latino groups (Puerto Rican, Cuban, Central American) have produced literature that is significant and growing in interest and intensity, Chicano literature usually includes only literature written by Mexicans in the United States and is normally taught with this demarcation in mind. Courses featuring a range of Latino literatures are indeed taught and should be encouraged, but this literature should be addressed under another rubric.

The use of the term "field" is drawn from anthropology because it connotes cultural domains in which paradigms are established and contested—that is, the creative space in which much cultural production occurs. I am indebted to Victor Turner's discussion of this and other concepts that are central to many of the arguments presented in this essay.

2. I explore the problems arising from constructing Chicano history from solely one region, such as Texas, in "An Utterance More Pure Than Word: Gender and the Corrido Tradition in Two Contemporary Chicano Poems," in *Feminist Measures: Soundings in Poetry and Theory*, ed. Lynn Keller and Cristanne Miller (Ann Arbor: University of Michigan Press, 1994), pp. 184–207.

3. See "An Utterance More Pure Than Word" for a discussion of the feminist implications of the study and production of the corrido form.

4.   a flower
inside the red
of an anger,

panaceas stroking
the inanity
of conferences
wherein we promenade
seeking messianic ones
to charismatically proclaim

that these moments
are more
than the anxieties
of our common lives

2. CHICANO POETRY AND THE POLITICAL AGE

1. Limón's periodization of the second phase of his Mexicano/
Chicano social drama corresponds roughly to the temporal divisions of Chicano
Movement and Postmovement mentioned at the beginning of this discussion. The
social drama framework, however, supersedes these kinds of divisions because it per-
mits discussion of politico-cultural action according to more fruitful theoretical and
practical rhetorical considerations.

2. The poem is reprinted in the text with its original spelling and syntax (my
translation):

A POEM BY ANTONIO'S MOTHER

I am going to write these lines
about what recently happened
They killed Antonio and Rito
in Albuquerque New Mexico

Nineteen hundred and seventy-two
The twenty-ninth of January
They killed Antonio and Rito
but they made their plans beforehand

They fell into the hands of men
with hard hearts
who killed them in Black Mesa
without any compassion

They shot Rito six times
they shot Antonio ten
they wanted to make sure
they would never get up again

They took them to Black Mesa
they betrayed them to kill them
so that they could
appear on a television program

Everyone knows
that they killed them in cold blood
the crime they accused them of

they have not yet been able to prove

The twenty-eighth of January
they made their plans
to commit this crime
and to be free of reprisals for their actions

These were two men
who did not fear death
they put their lives in danger
because they didn't want to see their people suffer

The men who killed them
were six inhumane men
but the blood they spilled
will be examined on their hands

There were two hundred people
who demanded the Truth
but they were before four people
covered with the cape of authority

Antonio did not need dynamite
to defend his rights
He had pen, paper, and his camera
to prove his deeds

They did not know that one day
they would have to be judged
and that before a just judge
they could not escape

We saw Anita's photograph
with her little son
And our hearts break
because his father could never see his son

I am not a poet, I am not anything
I am only a mother of a beloved son
and today I find myself
with my heart wounded

With this I say farewell
having so much more to say
and hoping that our beloved people
in the future will know how to unite.

3. Without recapitulating all the literature on the classic border corrido form, I will say that, like the ballad, the corrido tells a story that usually has a beginning, a

middle, and an end. The corrido is generally composed in octosyllabic quatrains and is sung in 3/4 or 6/8 meter. As in most oral and epic poems, moreover, the memory of the performer is assisted by formulaic phrases and formal introductions and closings and is structured in the common *a b c d* rhyme pattern.

4. Turner (1974, p. 169) describes three types of communitas: "(1) *existential or spontaneous* communitas, the direct, immediate, and total confrontation of human identities . . . (2) *normative* communitas, where, under the influence of time, the need to mobilize and organize resources to keep the members of a group alive and thriving . . . the original existential communitas is organized into a perduring social system . . . (3) *ideological* communitas, which is a label one can apply to a variety of utopian models or blueprints of societies believed by their authors to exemplify or supply the optimal conditions for existential communitas." I would argue that Mexican/ Chicano cultural performance, for the most part, operates within either normative or ideological communitas.

5. Turner (1974, p. 96) also explains that "because of the action of root paradigms in people's heads . . . [they] become objectified models for future behavior in the history of collectives such as churches or nations." Mexicans/Chicanos may not comprise a church or a nation in themselves, but because they are identified as a distinct racial/ethnic group within a larger dominant culture their status as a collective holds true, as does this action of root paradigms within their collective behavior.

6. For a fascinating analysis of the pachuco as popular cultural performance, see "The Pachuco's Flayed Hide: The Museum, Identity, and Buenas Garras," by Marcos Sánchez-Tranquilino and John Tagg, in *Chicano Art: Resistance and Affirmation, 1965–85,* ed. Richard Griswold del Castillo and Teresa McKenna et al., 97–108.

7. My translation:

> tired out by everything that day
> I sat down for a drink
> a cuba libre
> in a classy joint
> with delicately leafed green plants
> blossoming in all directions
> and picturesque windows
> brilliant mirrors
> and a polished wooden antique bar
>
> and I gazed out
> through elongated window structures
> framing like a picture
> the patio of the marketplace
> white, sun-bleached square tiles
> whereupon
> just one drink ago
> trotted the Indian feet clad in dusty shoes
> of that old man

who traversed the front door
of the costly Anglo-American bar—
I
for an instant
waiting for him to pass
and he
contained
in his clear thoughts
pushing with strong weathered brown arm
an ancient wooden cart
and in his left hand
a transistor radio
loudly playing polka music

and amazed
while just beginning to feel the buzz and warmth
I utter to myself out loud
"He's carrying a polka in his hand!"
and the anglo client seated next to me
glances over uncomprehendingly
and I think about Gregorio Cortez
and Américo Paredes
and that the defense of culture is permitted
and that calls for another drink
and another toast
and I say to myself in the mirror
"That's all!"
and I drink my drink

3. "ON LIES, SECRETS, AND SILENCE"

1. Rodriguez has since published another autobiographical text, *Days of Obligation: An Argument with My Father* (New York: Viking, 1992). Analysis of how this later work fits with the first one is needed, although it is not within the project of this chapter.

2. The line of difference is fine but acute. Chatman (1978) argues that historical narrative is governed by truth, while fictional narrative is ruled by verisimilitude or what he calls a semblance of veracity. Others argue that all narrative is governed by the semblance of veracity.

3. Richard Rodriguez, *Hunger of Memory: The Education of Richard Rodriguez* (Toronto: Bantam, 1983). All subsequent references are from this edition and are followed by page numbers in the text.

4. Chatman offers an intriguing proposition regarding the inclusion of a covert narrator within a text containing an overt narrator. The corollary to be drawn leads

to the possibility of the inclusion of a covert audience as well. Thus, while uncovering the covert narrator, which I am attempting here, we can also discern a covert audience. Rodriguez overtly states that he writes the autobiography to an Anglo American audience as a confession and a plea for forgiveness. The covert audience is, by contrast, the non-Anglo readership to whom the text is presented, not in supplication, but in hostility. Although it is not within the purview of this chapter to follow the implications of these observations, the issue bears scrutiny.

5. It is important to note that in recent years Rodriguez has become a public spokesperson and advocate for gay rights. His increasing public identification with the gay community suggests much about my argument here.

6. *I Know Why the Caged Bird Sings* (Toronto: Bantam Books, 1971); *The Names* (New York: Harper Colophon Books, 1976); *The Woman Warrior: Memoirs of a Girlhood among Ghosts* (New York: Vintage Books, 1977). All subsequent references are to these editions and are followed by page numbers in the text.

7. Chatman (1978, p. 146) uses this quotation as an epigraph to his Chapter 4: "Discourse: Nonnarrated Stories." The application was so apt that it demanded repeating.

4. POWER REVERSALS AND THE COMIC

1. Rolando Hinojosa-Smith, *Estampas del valle y otras obras: Sketches of the Valley and Other Works* (Berkeley: Quinto Sol Publications, 1973). All Spanish citations from the novel are from this edition. All subsequent references appear with appropriate page numbers in the text.

2. Because much of Hinojosa's humor is predicated on wordplay and manipulation of discourses, the fact that the translation included in the Quinto Sol edition left much to be desired is of acute importance. Hinojosa has since rectified the situation by publishing his own translation of the novel ten years after its first publication under the new title *The Valley* (Tempe, Ariz.: Bilingual Press/Editorial Bilingüe, 1983). All English translations are taken from this edition, and subsequent references are followed by appropriate page numbers in the text.

3. The literature on comedy is too extensive to recount here. Some important statements on the issue include Erasmus, *In Praise of Folly* (1992); Wimsatt, *The Idea of Comedy* (1969); Carlson, *The Benign Humorists* (1975); Caputi, *Buffo: The Genius of Vulgar Comedy* (1978); and Simon, *The Labyrinth of the Comic* (1985).

4. In *Rites and Witnesses, Mi querido Rafa*, and *Partners in Crime*, Hinojosa explores the discourses of power in Anglo Texas society in great detail. We need only reflect on the first chapter of *Rites and Witnesses*, in which Noddy Perkins and his fellow KBC (Klail, Blanchard, Cooke) directors consider the pros and cons of including Jehú Malacara within the bank hierarchy. In opposition to this conversation and others like it are Jehú's letters to Rafe Buenrostro in *Mi querido Rafa*, in which Jehú dissects the

machinations of the bank's directors and his growing relationship to them as a new-comer and, most importantly, as a Mexican within an Anglo structure.

5. One also could argue that Hinojosa creates a form of communitas with his au-dience through his narrative technique. Turner (1969, pp. 131–132) explains this com-plex term as "a relationship between concrete, historical, idiosyncratic individuals. . . . A direct, immediate and total confrontation of human identities." A relationship is cemented between the characters in Belken County and the audience. Where the nar-rator leaves important information unsaid, the force of the communitas identification fills the lacunae. In this way, Hinojosa links together the seemingly disparate elements of his narrative. This self-conscious fragmentation is addressed at greater length in the following section.

6. Simon (1985, p. 3) notes that "comic theory is an incongruous mixture of ap-proaches and miscellaneous assortment of arguments, many of them simple repeti-tions of conventional wisdom or straightforward attacks on the conventional wisdom, some of them extraordinary in their intellectual rigor and imaginative insight." Therefore, the task of separating out useful guides to this critical issue is truly labyrinthine. Yet one can unearth provocative texts that propel the discussion further. With this caveat, this essay relies heavily on statements by theorists such as Luigi Pi-randello, Suzanne Langer, and M. M. Bakhtin, who are sometimes considered mar-ginal to the classic discourses on comedy, but who expand the dialogue on the issue.

7. Luigi Pirandello, *On Humor,* trans. A. Iliano and D. P. Testa (Chapel Hill: Uni-versity of North Carolina Press, 1974), p. xi. All subsequent references are taken from this edition and are followed by appropriate page numbers in the text.

8. The choice of the name is significant since Romeo is Hinojosa's own middle name. One can infer that the strategy here is to call attention to the blurring of boundaries between fact and truth and, by extension, between fiction and reality.

9. Bakhtin (1981, p. 84) explains that "we will give the name *chronotope* (literally, 'time space') to the intrinsic connectedness of temporal and spatial relationships that are artistically expressed in literature. . . . What counts for us is the fact that it ex-presses the inseparability of space and time (time as the fourth dimension of space)." In addition, texts can contain a multitude of chronotopes.

10. Viola Barragán, like Rafe and Jehú, acquires experience outside the Valley. Just like them, she emerges as a survivor, indicating her strength and resilience. Moreover, we learn in *Rites and Witnesses* that she holds power in the community. In an interview I conducted with Hinojosa on May 27, 1988, he indicated that he wanted to continue the regenerative mode begun in *Partners in Crime* by choosing Viola as the root for that renewal in his next novel. This choice would point to a shift from patriarchal author-ity to female power and would appropriately epitomize the change and strength evi-dent in the survival of Mexican Valley culture. Hinojosa's *Becky and Her Friends,* how-ever, focuses on Becky Escobar's decision to reaffirm her Mexican identity, participate in Valley politics, and establish her own business under the tutelage of Viola. This novel, it appears, further explores the regeneration of Valley culture, which is at the core of the process of death and renewal that is the nexus of Hinojosa's novelistic project.

5. ENGENDERING THE BORDER

1. Sonia Saldívar-Hull (1991) is persuasive in her argument that liberal Anglo American feminists have colonized women's history. Indeed, her criticism of Kristeva's attempt to theorize women's time is well taken. Kristeva's formulations can be perceived as overly simple constructions of significant moments in feminist history. Whose history is she speaking about? Yet, although I agree with Saldívar-Hull's fundamental argument, I am using Kristeva here because of her attempt to theorize the intersection of body, sex, and symbol, to which she brings the emplotment of history, "the interweaving of history and geography" (Kristeva 1988, p. 31). The importance of her theory is that it might provide an alternative language to speak about Chicanas' insertion into history, how indeed to understand the continuity of Chicana struggle that has been overlooked by the patriarchy in its constructions of Chicano history. Women's time involves the connectedness of events, as well as the simultaneity of struggle. This is the subject of this chapter.

2. The choice of Sara Estela Ramírez, Cherríe Moraga, and Pat Mora for this chapter was made in order to illustrate the connection of historical events through each writer's similar, yet different political activism. They are poets, essayists, and activists. Theirs is a distinctive fusion of political action and aesthetics—their writing explores the intersection of body, sex, and symbol. Although other Chicana writers and works would indeed also show these elements, this chapter focuses on only these three as an illustration of the active emplotment of history that is central to Chicana literature.

3. Pat Mora's collection of essays *Nepantla: Essays from the Land in the Middle* (1993) deals with issues of cultural conservation and aesthetics. Like Ramírez and Moraga, Mora uses the essay genre to challenge official versions of culture, gender, and sexuality.

Bibliography

Acosta, Oscar Zeta. 1974. *Autobiography of a Brown Buffalo*. London: Charisma Books.

Alarcón, Norma, ed. 1986. *Third Woman: Texas and More*. Bloomington: Indiana University Press.

Alurista. 1970. "Poem in Lieu of Preface." *Aztlán: Chicano Journal of the Social Sciences and the Arts* 1, no. 1 (Spring), ix.

———. 1971. *Floricanto en Aztlán*. Los Angeles: Chicano Studies Center Publications, University of California, Los Angeles.

———. 1972. *Nationchild Plumaroja*. San Diego, Calif.: Toltecas en Aztlán Centro Cultural de la Raza.

———. 1976. *Timespace Huracán*. Albuquerque: Pajarito Publications.

Anaya, Rudolfo A. 1972. *Bless Me, Ultima*. Berkeley, Calif.: Quinto Sol Publications.

———. 1976. *Heart of Aztlán*. Berkeley, Calif.: Editorial Justa Publications.

———. 1979. *Tortuga*. Berkeley, Calif.: Editorial Justa Publications.

———. 1982. *The Silence of the Llano*. Berkeley, Calif.: TQS Publishing.

———. 1992. *Albuquerque*. Albuquerque: University of New Mexico Press.

Anaya, Rudolfo A., and José Griego y Maestas, eds. 1980. *Hispanic Folktales of the Southwest: Cuentos Hispanoamericanos*. Santa Fe: Museum of New Mexico Press.

Angelou, Maya. 1971. *I Know Why the Caged Bird Sings*. Toronto: Bantam Books.

Anzaldúa, Gloria. 1987. *Borderlands/La Frontera*. San Francisco: Aunt Lute Books.

Arias, Ron. 1975. *The Road to Tamazunchale*. Reno, Nev.: West Coast Poetry Review. Reprinted 1987.

Baca, Jimmy Santiago. 1979. *Immigrants in Our Own Land*. Baton Rouge: Louisiana State University Press.

Bakhtin, M. M. 1981. *The Dialogic Imagination: Four Essays*. Ed. Michael Holquist; trans. Caryl Emerson and Michael Holquist. Austin: University of Texas Press.

———. 1984. *Rabelais and His World*. Trans. Helene Iswolsky. Bloomington: Indiana University Press.

Baldwin, James. 1988. "A Talk to Teachers." In *Multi-cultural Literacy*, ed. Rick Simonson and Scott Walker, pp. 3–12. Saint Paul: Graywolf Press.

Barrio, Raymond. 1969. *The Plum Plum Pickers*. Sunnyvale, Calif.: Ventura Press.

Bruce-Novoa, Juan. 1980. *Chicano Authors: Inquiry by Interview*. Austin: University of Texas Press.

————. 1982. *Chicano Poetry: A Response to Chaos.* Austin: University of Texas Press.

Burke, Kenneth. 1966. *Language as Symbolic Action: Essays on Life, Literature, and Method.* Berkeley: University of California Press.

Calvino, Italo. 1982. *The Uses of Literature.* Ed. Patrick Creagh. New York: Harcourt, Brace, Jovanovich, Publishers.

Caputi, Anthony E. 1978. *Buffo: The Genius of Vulgar Comedy.* Detroit: Wayne State University Press.

Carlson, Richard. 1975. *The Benign Humorists.* Hamden, Conn.: Archon Books.

Castillo, Ana. 1984. *Women Are Not Roses.* Houston, Tex.: Arte Público Press.

————. 1990. *Sapogonia.* Tempe, Ariz.: Bilingual Review Press.

Castillo, Pedro, and Albert Camarillo. 1972. *Furia y muerte: Los bandidos chicanos.* Los Angeles: Chicano Studies Center Publications, University of California, Los Angeles.

Cervantes, Lorna Dee. 1981. *Emplumada.* Pittsburgh, Penn.: University of Pittsburgh Press.

Chatman, Seymour. 1978. *Story and Discourse: Narrative Structure in Fiction and Film.* Ithaca, N.Y.: Cornell University Press.

Chávez, Denise. 1986. *The Last of the Menu Girls.* Houston, Tex.: Arte Público Press.

Cisneros, Sandra. 1983. *The House on Mango Street.* Houston, Tex.: Arte Público Press.

————. 1991. *Woman Hollering Creek.* New York: Random House.

Cooper, Lane, ed. 1960. *The Rhetoric of Aristotle.* Englewood Cliffs, N.J.: Prentice Hall.

Corpi, Lucha. 1980. *Palabras de mediodía: Noon Words.* Berkeley, Calif.: El Fuego de Aztlán Publications.

Cota-Cárdenas, Margarita. 1977. *Noches despertando inconciencias.* Tucson, Ariz.: Scorpion Press.

de Hoyos, Angela. 1975. *Arise, Chicano! and Other Poems.* San Antonio, Tex.: M & A Editions.

Delgado, Abelardo. 1969. *Chicano: 25 Pieces of a Chicano Mind.* Denver, Colo.: Barrio Publications.

"Editorial." 1973. *El Grito del Norte* (Española, N. Mex.), January 29, p. 4.

Elizondo, Sergio. 1972. *Perros y antiperros.* Berkeley, Calif.: Quinto Sol Publications.

Enzensberger, Hans Magnus. 1974. *The Consciousness Industry: On Literature, Politics, and the Media.* New York: Seabury Press.

Erasmus, Desiderius. 1992. *In Praise of Folly.* Albuquerque: American Institute of Psychology.

Foucault, Michel. 1977. *Language, Counter-memory, Practice: Selected Essays and Interviews.* Ithaca, N.Y.: Cornell University Press.

Frye, Northrop. 1957. *Anatomy of Criticism.* Princeton, N.J.: Princeton University Press.

Galarza, Ernesto. 1971. *Barrio Boy.* Notre Dame, Ind.: University of Notre Dame Press.

García, Ricardo. 1973. *Selected Poetry.* Berkeley, Calif.: Quinto Sol Publications.

Gardner, John. 1977. *On Moral Fiction.* New York: Basic Books.

Gates, Henry Louis, Jr. 1992. *Loose Canons: Notes on the Culture Wars.* New York: Oxford University Press.

Gómez-Peña, Guillermo. 1988. "Documented/Undocumented." In *The Graywolf Annual Five: Multicultural Literacy,* ed. Rick Simonson and Scott Walker, pp. 127–134. Saint Paul: Graywolf Press.

Gómez-Quiñones, Juan. 1974. *5th and Grande Vista.* New York: Editorial Mensaje.

———. 1977. *On Culture.* Popular Series no. 1. Los Angeles: Chicano Studies Center Publications, University of California, Los Angeles.

———. 1990. *Chicano Politics: Reality and Promise, 1940–1990.* Albuquerque: University of New Mexico Press.

Graff, Gerald. 1979. *Literature against Itself: Literary Ideas in Modern Society.* Chicago: University of Chicago Press.

Hernández, Inés. 1984. "Sara Estela Ramírez: The Early Twentieth Century Texas-Mexican Poet." Ph.D. dissertation, University of Houston.

———. 1989. "Sara Estela Ramírez: Sembradora." *Legacy: A Journal of Nineteenth Century American Women Writers* 6, no. 1 (Spring), 13–26.

Herrera-Sobek, María, and Helena María Viramontes. 1988. *Chicana Creativity and Criticism: Charting New Frontiers in American Literature.* Houston, Tex.: Arte Público Press.

Hinojosa-Smith, Rolando. 1973. *Estampas del valle y otras obras: Sketches of the Valley and Other Works.* Berkeley, Calif.: Quinto Sol Publications.

———. 1976. *Klail City y sus alrededores.* Havana, Cuba: Casa de las Américas.

———. 1977. *Generaciones y semblanzas.* Berkeley, Calif.: Editorial Justa Publications.

———. 1978. *Korean Love Songs.* Berkeley, Calif.: Editorial Justa Publications.

———. 1981. *Mi querido Rafa.* Houston, Tex.: Arte Público Press.

———. 1982. *Rites and Witnesses.* Houston, Tex.: Arte Público Press.

———. 1983. *The Valley.* Tempe, Ariz.: Bilingual Press/Editorial Bilingüe.

———. 1985a. *Dear Rafe.* Houston, Tex.: Arte Público Press.

———. 1985b. *Partners in Crime.* Houston, Tex.: Arte Público Press.

———. 1985c. "A Voice of One's Own." In *The Rolando Hinojosa Reader: Essays Historical and Critical,* ed. José David Saldívar, pp. 11–17. Houston, Tex.: Arte Público Press.

———. 1986. *Claros varones de Belken: Fair Gentlemen of Belken County.* Tempe, Ariz.: Bilingual Press/Editorial Bilingüe.

———. 1989. *Becky and Her Friends.* Houston, Tex.: Arte Público Press.

———. 1993. *Useless Servants.* Houston, Tex.: Arte Público Press.

Huerta, Jorge. 1982. *Chicano Theater: Themes and Forms.* Tempe, Ariz.: Bilingual Press/Editorial Bilingüe.

Islas, Arturo. 1985. *The Rain God: A Desert Tale.* Stanford, Calif.: Alexandrian Press.

———. 1990a. *Migrant Souls.* New York: Morrow.

———. 1990b. "On the Bridge, at the Border: Migrants and Immigrants." Fifth annual Ernesto Galarza memorial lecture, Stanford Center for Chicano Research, Stanford, Calif.

Jameson, Frederic. 1971. *Marxism and Form: Twentieth-Century Dialectical Theories of Literature.* Princeton: Princeton University Press.

Jiménez, Francisco, ed. 1979. *The Identification and Analysis of Chicano Literature.* Tempe, Ariz.: Bilingual Press.

Kermode, Frank. 1980. "Secrets and Narrative Sequence." In *On Narrative,* ed. W. J. T. Mitchell, pp. 79–97. Chicago: University of Chicago Press.

Kingston, Maxine Hong. 1977. *The Woman Warrior: Memoirs of a Girlhood among Ghosts.* New York: Vintage Books.

Kristeva, Julia. 1981. "Women's Time." In *Feminist Theory: A Critique of Ideology,* ed. Nannerk O. Keohane and Michelle Z. Rosaldo et al., pp. 31–53. Chicago: University of Chicago Press.

Langer, Suzanne. 1953. *Feeling and Form.* New York: Charles Scribner's Sons.

Leal, Luis, et al., eds. 1982. *A Decade of Chicano Literature.* Santa Barbara: Editorial La Causa.

Lentricchia, Frank. 1980. *After the New Criticism.* Chicago: University of Chicago Press.

———. 1983. *Criticism and Social Change.* Chicago: University of Chicago Press.

Limón, José E. 1973. "Stereotyping and Chicano Resistance: An Historical Dimension." *Aztlán: International Journal of Chicano Studies Research* 4, no. 2 (Fall), 257–270.

———. 1986a. *Mexican Ballads, Chicano Epic: History, Social Dramas, and Poetic Persuasions.* SCCR Working Paper no. 14. Stanford, Calif.: Stanford Center for Chicano Research.

———. 1986b. *The Return of the Mexican Ballad: Américo Paredes and His Anthropological Text in Persuasive Political Performance.* SCCR Working Paper no. 16. Stanford, Calif.: Stanford Center for Chicano Research.

———. 1992. *Mexican Ballads, Chicano Poems.* Berkeley: University of California Press.

———. 1994. *Dancing with the Devil: Society and Cultural Poetics in Mexican-American South Texas.* Madison: University of Wisconsin Press.

Madrid-Barela, Arturo. 1973. "In Search of the Authentic Pachuco." *Aztlán: International Journal of Chicano Studies Research* 4, no. 1 (Spring), 31–60.

Magón, Ricardo Flores. 1980. "A la mujer." In *Mexican Women in the United States: Struggles Past and Present,* ed. Magdalena Mora and Adelaida del Castillo, pp. 160–162. Los Angeles: Chicano Studies Research Center Publications.

McWilliams, Carey. 1968. *North from Mexico.* Westport, Conn.: Greenwood Press.

Méndez, Miguel. 1975. *Peregrinos de Aztlán.* Tucson, Ariz.: Editorial Peregrinos.

Momaday, N. Scott. 1976. *The Names.* New York: Harper Colophon Books.

Mora, Pat. 1984. *Chants.* Houston, Tex.: Arte Público Press.

———. 1986. *Borders.* Houston, Tex.: Arte Público Press.

———. 1991. *Communion.* Houston, Tex.: Arte Público Press.

———. 1993. *Nepantla: Essays from the Land in the Middle.* Albuquerque: University of New Mexico Press.

Moraga, Cherríe. 1983. *Loving in the War Years: Lo que nunca pasó por sus labios.* Boston: South End Press.

———. 1986. *Giving Up the Ghost.* Albuquerque: West End Press.

Moraga, Cherríe, and Gloria Anzaldúa, eds. 1981. *This Bridge Called My Back: Writings by Radical Women of Color.* Watertown, Mass.: Persephone Press.

Morales, Alejandro. 1975. *Caras viejas y vino nuevo*. Mexico City: Editorial Joaquín Mortiz.

Morton, Carlos. 1983. *The Many Deaths of Danny Rosales and Other Plays*. Houston, Tex.: Arte Público Press.

Niggli, Josephina. 1945. *Mexican Village*. Chapel Hill: University of North Carolina Press.

Ong, Walter J. 1982. *Orality and Literacy: The Technologizing of the Word*. London, England: Methuen.

Paredes, Américo. 1958. *With His Pistol in His Hand: A Border Ballad and Its Hero*. Austin: University of Texas Press.

————. 1964. "Some Aspects of Folk Poetry." *Texas Studies in Literature and Language* 5, no. 2 (Summer), 213–225.

————. 1979. "The Folk Base of Chicano Literature." In *Modern Chicano Writers*, ed. Joseph Sommers and Tomás Ybarra-Frausto, pp. 4–17. Englewood Cliffs, N.J.: Prentice-Hall.

————. 1982. "Folklore, lo Mexicano, and Proverbs." In special issue on Mexican folklore and folk art in the United States, ed. Teresa McKenna: *Aztlán: International Journal of Chicano Studies Research* 13, nos. 1–2 (Spring–Fall), 1–11.

Peña, Manuel. 1982. "Folk Song and Social Change: Two Corridos as Interpretive Sources." *Aztlán: International Journal of Chicano Studies Research* 13, nos. 1–2, 13–38.

————. 1985. *The Texas-Mexican Conjunto: History of a Working-Class Music*. Austin: University of Texas Press.

Pirandello, Luigi. 1974. *On Humor*. Trans. A. Iliano and D. P. Testa. Chapel Hill: University of North Carolina Press.

Portillo-Trambley, Estela. 1975. *Rain of Scorpions*. Berkeley, Calif.: Tonatiuh International.

————. 1983. *Sor Juana and Other Plays*. Ypsilanti, Mich.: Bilingual Press.

Raíz fuerte que no se arranca. 1983. Memorial volume dedicated to Magdalena Mora. Los Angeles, Calif.: El Foro del Pueblo Publications.

Rebolledo, Tey Diana. 1989. "Tradition and Mythology: Signatures of Landscape in Chicana Literature." In *The Desert Is No Lady: Southwestern Landscapes in Women's Writing and Art*, ed. Vera Norwood and Janice Monk. New Haven: Yale University Press.

Revista Chicano-Riqueña. 1985. Special edition, "Tomás Rivera."

Rich, Adrienne. 1979. *On Lies, Secrets, and Silence: Selected Prose 1966–1978*. New York: W. W. Norton and Company.

————. 1986. *Blood, Bread, and Poetry: Selected Prose 1979–1985*. New York: W. W. Norton and Company.

Ríos, Alberto A. 1982. *Whispering to Fool the Wind*. Bronx, N.Y.: Sheep Meadow Press.

————. 1985a. *Five Indiscretions*. Bronx, N.Y.: Sheep Meadow Press.

————. 1985b. *The Iguana Killer*. Lewiston, Idaho: Blue Moon Press.

Rivera, Tomás. 1971. *Y no se lo tragó la tierra: And the Earth Did Not Part*. Berkeley, Calif.: Quinto Sol Publications.

Rodriguez, Richard. 1983. *Hunger of Memory: The Education of Richard Rodriguez*. Toronto: Bantam Books.

Romano-V., Octavio I. 1969. "Goodbye Revolution—Hello Slum." In *El Espejo: The Mirror,* ed. Octavio I. Romano-V., pp. 46–82. Berkeley, Calif.: Quinto Sol Publications.

Rosaldo, Renato. 1986. "Beyond the Rules of the Game." Unpublished ms.

Said, Edward. 1983. *The World, the Text, and the Critic.* Cambridge, Mass.: Harvard University Press.

Saldívar, José David, ed. 1985a. *The Rolando Hinojosa Reader: Essays Historical and Critical.* Houston, Tex.: Arte Público Press.

———. 1985b. "Rolando Hinojosa's Klail City Death Trip Series: A Critical Introduction." In *The Rolando Hinojosa Reader: Essays Historical and Critical,* ed. José David Saldívar, pp. 44–63. Houston, Tex.: Arte Público Press.

———. 1991. *The Dialectics of Our America: Genealogy, Cultural Critique, and Literary History.* Durham, N.C.: Duke University Press.

Saldívar, José David, and Héctor Calderón, eds. 1991. *Criticism in the Borderlands: Studies in Chicano Literature, Culture, and Ideology.* Durham, N.C.: Duke University Press.

Saldívar, Ramón. 1990. *Chicano Narrative: The Dialectics of Difference.* Madison: University of Wisconsin Press.

———. 1991. "Narrative, Ideology, and the Reconstruction of American Literary History." In *Criticism in the Borderlands: Studies in Chicano Literature, Culture, and Ideology,* ed. José David Saldívar and Héctor Calderón, pp. 11–20. Durham, N.C.: Duke University Press.

Saldívar-Hull, Sonia. 1991. "Feminism on the Border: From Gender Politics to Geopolitics." In *Criticism in the Borderlands: Studies in Chicano Literature, Culture, and Ideology,* ed. José David Saldívar and Héctor Calderón, pp. 203–220. Durham, N.C.: Duke University Press.

Sánchez, Marta. 1985. *Contemporary Chicana Poetry: An Approach to an Emerging Literature.* Berkeley: University of California Press.

Sánchez, Ricardo. 1971. *Canto y grito mi liberación.* El Paso, Tex.: Mixtla Publications.

———. 1976. *Hechizospells.* Los Angeles: Chicano Studies Center Publications, University of California, Los Angeles.

Sánchez, Rosaura. 1985. "From Heterogeneity to Contradiction: Hinojosa's Novel." In *The Rolando Hinojosa Reader: Essays Historical and Critical,* ed. José David Saldívar, pp. 76–100. Houston, Tex.: Arte Público Press.

Sánchez-Tranquilino, Marcos, and John Tagg. 1991. "The Pachuco's Flayed Hide: The Museum, Identity, and Buenas Garras." In *Chicano Art: Resistance and Affirmation, 1965–85,* ed. Richard Griswold del Castillo and Teresa McKenna et al., pp. 97–108. Los Angeles: Wight Art Gallery, University of California, Los Angeles.

Scholes, Robert, and Robert Kellogg. 1966. *The Nature of Narrative.* New York: Oxford University Press.

Simon, Richard K. 1985. *The Labyrinth of the Comic: Theory and Practice from Fielding to Freud.* Tallahassee: Florida State University Press.

Sommers, Joseph. 1979. "Critical Approaches to Chicano Literature." In *Modern Chicano Writers,* ed. Joseph Sommers and Tomás Ybarra-Frausto, pp. 31–40. Englewood Cliffs, N.J.: Prentice-Hall.

Sommers, Joseph, and Tomás Ybarra-Frausto, eds. 1979. *Modern Chicano Writers.* Englewood Cliffs, N.J.: Prentice-Hall.

Soto, Gary. 1977. *The Elements of San Joaquín.* Pittsburgh, Penn.: University of Pittsburgh Press.

———. 1978. *The Tale of Sunlight.* Pittsburgh, Penn.: University of Pittsburgh Press.

Tafolla, Carmen. 1983. *Curandera.* San Antonio, Tex.: M & A Editions.

Turner, Victor. 1969. *The Ritual Process: Structure and Anti-Structure.* Ithaca, N.Y.: Cornell University Press.

———. 1974. *Dramas, Fields, and Metaphors: Symbolic Action in Human Society.* Ithaca, N.Y.: Cornell University Press.

———. 1981. "Social Dramas and Stories about Them." In *On Narrative,* ed. W. J. T. Mitchell, pp. 137–164. Chicago: University of Chicago Press.

Valdez, Luis. 1971. *Actos.* Fresno, Calif.: Cucaracha Press.

———. 1992. *Zoot Suit.* Houston, Tex.: Arte Público Press.

Vásquez, Richard. 1970. *Chicano.* New York: Doubleday.

Venegas, Daniel. 1984. *Las aventuras de Don Chipote, o cuando los pericos mamen.* Houston, Tex.: Arte Público Press.

Vigil, Evangelina. 1984. *Woman of Her Word.* Houston, Tex.: Arte Público Press.

———. 1985. *Thirty an' Seen a Lot.* Houston, Tex.: Arte Público Press.

Villanueva, Tino. 1972. *Hay Otra Voz Poems: 1968–1971.* New York: Editorial Mensaje.

Villarreal, José Antonio. 1959. *Pocho.* New York: Doubleday.

Viramontes, Helena. 1990. *The Moths.* Houston, Tex.: Arte Público Press.

West, Cornel. 1993. *Race Matters.* Boston: Beacon Press.

Wimsatt, William K. 1969. *The Idea of Comedy: Essays on Prose and Verse.* Englewood Cliffs, N.J.: Prentice-Hall.

Zamora, Bernice. 1976. *Restless Serpents.* Menlo Park, Calif.: Diseños Literarios.

Zamora, Emilio. 1980. "Sara Estela Ramírez: Una rosa roja en el movimiento." In *Mexican Women in the United States: Struggles Past and Present,* ed. Magdalena Mora and Adelaida del Castillo, pp. 163–169. Los Angeles: Chicano Studies Research Center Publications.

Index